Authentic Democracy

Authentic Democracy

HOW PROXY VOTING CAN RENEW OUR DEMOCRACY

———

Michael Parides

ISBN-13: 978-0-578-60423-7

"A society grows great when old men plant trees whose shade they know they will never sit in."

—OLD GREEK PROVERB

Drawing by Sarah Carroll

Table of Contents

Introduction

———

THERE IS AN UNRECOGNIZED PROBLEM in the structure of 21st democracies which leaves a large segment of the population without representation. In the United States, fully 25% of these United States citizens are left without the right to an equal vote and therefore without representation and influence in the direction and decisions of federal, state, and local governments.

This group of unrepresented citizens are minors, citizens under the age of 18. This gap in representation ultimately results in government policies which are made with far lower focus on the impact on this group than would be the case if they were fully represented as citizens. This creates a range of government policies that have a detrimental impact on the entire course of their lives and those of their support groups - mostly young families. Beyond the direct government policy decisions, the relative disregard for their interests in policy decisions is changing the future of American culture and society.

If the needs of these citizens were included equally, most of the largest and most problematic national issues would be approached quite differently by our federal, state, and local government representatives. There would also be a change over time to the judiciary, causing a delayed but important secondary effect broadly across American culture. The National Debt, National Defense, Foreign Policy, Social Security, Public Education and Higher Education, Public Pension liabilities – all of these and many other areas would be approached differently by representatives if these citizens were viewed as true constituents with the same voting power as other citizens.

This does not propose that minors themselves would vote. Instead, a proxy vote that represents the minor would be shared by the parents or guardians. Proxy votes are well proven in their use in shareholder votes for public corporations and included in Robert's Rules, the widely used manual on parliamentary procedure. The process and logistics do not require great complexity or cost in comparison to other voting mechanisms and are well cost-justified compared to the high importance and value of the vote in an authentic democracy.

Beyond the costs of additional process management and logistics, there is little reason to systematically exclude the interests of any subset of citizens, least of all the group which is often and accurately proclaimed as heir to the nation's future. The discussion which follows will provide the evidence on how this gap has already fostered the creation and growth of many large problems which will continue to increase until we establish balanced and fair representation.

The first line of the Preamble to the Constitution might be the most clear and powerful lead sentence ever written, building from one phrase to the next. It defines the overarching objectives and scope of the document and the foundational principles underlying American democracy:

> *We the People of the United States, in Order to form a more perfect Union, establish Justice, insure domestic Tranquility, provide for the common defense, promote the general Welfare, and secure the Blessings of Liberty to ourselves and our Posterity, do ordain and establish this Constitution for the United States of America.*

The nation was formed, and the Constitution written to serve The People. It was initially not intended with everyone in mind, but we now unequivocally interpret and enforce it to include all citizens. The journey to reach full representation has been long and difficult, often tragic; with many steps to remove the many barriers which excluded citizens from the vote and from their fair representation as citizens.

Those barriers dropped one step at a time - wealth, religion, race, ethnicity, and gender. Each of the former barriers were once believed by the majority of existing voters as reasonable, and the result of exclusion for the disenfranchised group was always highly detrimental. The best evidence of the immense power of that representation is the vast improvements for each group after achieving the vote. These improvements were often delayed, but ultimately the expansion of the vote has always led to economic, societal and quality of life improvements for the newly enfranchised group; unleashing the potential for each group and ultimately improving the lives of all Americans. Each improvement was a step toward the most simple, but elegant and beautiful aspect of democracy; empowering each individual with equal power to optimize their world towards their best interest, and towards their belief of what is best for the nation.

There is no logical reason that is consistent with the inclusive concept of democracy that would leave 25% of the population without representation. Several of the most critical decisions currently facing the nation have a much higher impact on minors and their families than on other citizens. Chapter 2 below will provide several areas where this gap is problematic, but here are two easy and obvious examples at the federal level: 1) The National Debt growth and continuing deficit spending is a decision that eventually will leave the negative result squarely upon this group. Without the franchise, there is no representation for the generation who inevitably inherits this debt and will have ultimate responsibility to continue to carry it. The vote would provide a balancing force to represent their interests on this highly political issue which is easy for U.S. representatives to neglect under the current mix of constituent priorities. 2) Social Security and Medicare, have grown steadily over the years, each serving as transfer payments from younger Americans, including the working parents of minors, to older Americans. While Social Security is, in theory, a partial return of prior invested funds, it is not accurate that the older Americans invested the level of funds they are receiving. In the case of Medicare, the difference between payments into the system and benefits is even more dramatic. Together these programs draw resources from younger citizens, including the families of minor children, and transfers these resources and wealth to older Americans. Since older Americans are, on average, substantially wealthier than those in the child rearing stage of their lives, it is effectively a highly regressive tax on the families of those minors. Beyond the issue of the immediate regressive transfer, it is also noteworthy that the Social Security system is known to be approaching a funding gap that will make it unable to provide the promised benefits at the time when today's minors are scheduled to receive benefits. It should not be surprising that this is a longstanding and unresolved issue. It will remain neglected without representation for minors, continuously pushed forward until it becomes a crisis.

At the state and local level, there are two obvious examples: 1) Unfunded public pension liabilities have grown to extremely high levels through the generosity of government leaders who are able to promise pension benefits to government employees without paying the political price of raising taxes. This is an unseen form of deficit spending – adding to the other, more visible deficit spending. These pensions will eventually require higher taxation on a future generation to continue to support the promises made in the past, and still being made today, by our government representatives. The growing debts will fall squarely on future generations, but government representatives are cleverly aware that they are not required to address these issues since the debt will transfer to a group that is not their constituency, since they are not represented through a vote. 2) Education funding and influence over education policy are both critically important to minors and those that represent them, and the decisions that government takes on education will affect the entire course of their lives. The nation's level of annual investment in public primary and secondary education is huge, ($550 Billion, nearly as much as Social Security), but the level of political influence of minors and their families over the local decisions of the representatives is not nearly proportional to their size, nor to its importance to their futures. Expanding the vote would shift power to those who care most about the value and results of public education and place it where it should be – serving the educational needs of the minors and their families.

At the broader level of society, higher education expenses have grown far above inflation over the past 30 years, with no end in sight. Families of minors are required to contribute a lifetime of savings or saddle themselves with a load of debt to support a future for their children, or the student must carry that debt through young adulthood. These costs can be the largest expense of a lifetime, consuming all discretionary income for the middle class and creating a burdensome debt that families will carry for many years; despite this there are no serious government initiatives to properly understand and limit the drivers of cost. In fact, economic analysis makes clear that government intervention to date has directly served to fuel the increase in cost by freely providing loan funds in a method that encourages the price increases, because it makes the buyers, (students and families), less price sensitive.

This lack of voting representation of minors was less of a problem in the past. Before the introduction of reliable birth control, the full population of adults had a greater shared interest in the priorities and needs of minors. Family size was larger, so citizens of voting age without children would at least have more frequent contact through siblings or other relatives with children, supporting that shared interest. Another factor that has changed is the dramatic rise of the proportion of voting Americans who are older and disconnected from child rearing. Before the increase in longevity, the majority of adult population was much closer to child rearing age. There was simply no group that approached the size and power of our current elderly population. This will only grow to be a larger and even more powerful group in the future. Imagine life expectancy expanding and the number of births

declining. That society would have a very small minority of adults raising families, who will be carrying the future with limited funds and
votes, and therefore limited political power, completely overwhelmed
by an older population with its votes, financial resources and the political power that is developed over a lifetime.

The symptoms of this lack of representation are all around us but
because the underlying causes changed over a long period, it takes
careful review and reflection to diagnose the connection to many
challenges faced by families. Adopting the proxy vote for children will
be a difficult idea to promote since the citizens most effected, minors
and their families, are themselves not aware that this gap is a problem
and not in a good position to advocate for change. It will require many
people to understand the issue and a few willing to evangelize the idea
into a movement. The past organized movements to extend the vote
to all citizens took decades; from the abolition movement to achieving the vote for African-Americans through the 15th Amendment,
and from the early call for women's rights to the movement leading to
women's suffrage and the 19th Amendment. It was a long process from
the original formation of groups attempting to enlighten others on
the need for change, followed by periods of extensive conflict, before
finally reaching legislation. We should not wait that long. It is not clear
what dystopian future awaits future generations if there is no course
correction.

The old Greek proverb, "A society grows great when old men plant
trees whose shade they will never know" is simple wisdom about the
importance of selfless giving from one generation to another. (The
same wisdom is repeated using different words in other cultures.) It has
been this spirit of selflessness and love for others, from parents to children, from soldiers in battle to their family and friends at home, from
the founding patriots to the next generations of Americans, which
leads to a society of freedom, justice and prosperity (with more work
to be done to get it right and make it universal!). The mirror of that
simple wisdom is also true: "a society will wither when old men (and

women) are unwilling to plant trees whose shade they will not know." A society so focused on today's personal benefits of security, wealth, pleasure, envy, and all the rest, at the expense of future generations, must inevitably decline. If the future of the nation matters to you, please take the time to read on and consider and reflect on the proxy vote's importance to our future and to the lives of all Americans.

CHAPTER 1

Adjusting to Change

———

The soft-minded man always fears change. He feels
security in the status quo, and he has an almost morbid
fear of the new. For him, the greatest pain
is the pain of a new idea.

—MARTIN LUTHER KING JR.

THIS IS A TIME OF change and there are many yet unimagined changes on the horizon. This prediction will **always** prove true and should be obvious to observant citizens of the 21st century. Despite our understanding that change will come, we imagine the future as an extension of now, and tend to overestimate our ability to predict the nature of change that will likely come. The improvements in access to information and communications technologies, along with a comparatively stable present day, encourages overconfidence about our ability to foresee how the future will unfold. These predictions, however well researched or backed by expert opinion, should not be relied upon. Consider that among the most important changes of the 20th century, very few were predicted by even the most informed perspectives of the 19th century. Pick the category - technology, medicine, war, politics, economics, social change – few of the most important changes were anticipated, and many were beyond imagination. The fact is that the changes that cause the greatest shifts in our complex world are simply not well predicted. They emerge and suddenly thrust society towards rapid adjustment, or for those that don't adjust, towards deterioration and decline. The size and increasing complexity of the world suggests that the future will bring more change, not less.

As with biological evolution, the civilizations and societies that adapt to the shocks of change are the ones that will survive and thrive. The history of the rise and fall of many civilizations throughout human history offers empirical proof that changes in conditions require adaptation or inevitable decline will follow, and that survival for civilizations is analogous in many ways to the process for biological systems. Unlike biological systems which don't make a conscious decision to adapt beyond simple survival, civilizations are capable of recognizing the changing environment. They can actively choose to adapt to the new reality or to act to modify the environment. For civilizations, recognizing the change and taking action, i.e. adapting, means survival, just as trusting in past success, seeking to remain static, and holding tightly to old behavior leads to failure.

This chapter describes several broad changes which have dramatically altered the environment of the nation, threatening our democratic process and therefore the future of our society and our nation. These changes combine to significantly reduce the representation in government for the needs and issues of those who will carry the future of our nation - minors and their families. These changes have developed over the past century, and have accelerated over the last 25 years. They are hiding in plain sight. That is, the symptoms are known separately and often discussed, but surprisingly, they are not well recognized as correlated, nor recognized as jointly creating a broader systemic problem. They show no signs of abating or reversing; the trend is in fact towards increase, possibly acceleration, and they threaten to take us into dangerous territory. The underlying systematic changes themselves are largely outside of our control. However, it is how we choose to adapt that will determine the future of the nation.

For simplicity these changes are grouped below into four categories of change:

1. **Demographic changes** have reduced the voting power of young families. The two main contributors to this are the 1) the increase in longevity which has created a large older population; a large group that is often less connected with the needs and concerns of young families, and is adapting to its own very different and pressing set of priorities; and 2) the increase in selective parenthood, through more effective birth control causing smaller extended families, and a larger adult population choosing to forgo parenthood. These child-free adults, combined with smaller extended families results in an adult population that can no longer represent an equal awareness and concern for the needs of citizens who are minors.

2. **The massive growth in the government** in the United States over the past century has vastly increased the importance of the power of the vote. This is not simply growth corresponding to growth with the economy, but rather it is growth in its size relative to the nation's economy and to gross national product. The most accessible data for comparison is at the federal government level which has grown from expenditures of less than 3 % of national output in 1900 to 24 % in 2012. (Schuler, 2014)[1] This is not simply a phenomenon of the federal government, but is happening concurrently with growth at the state and local levels. Beyond gathering and distributing economic resources, the government has also grown to establish laws and regulations that mediate and influence all areas of citizen's lives. Government representatives, agencies, and the courts determine the winners and losers, increasing the importance of government in each successive election cycle. This discussion will not suggest a method for government to be limited, nor does it propose continued growth by adding more resources to

better manage the growth, but instead simply highlights that the stakes are high and growing.

3. **The expansion of large and powerful organizations** in the United States and throughout the world increasingly compete with all citizens to influence government representatives and voters. This results in diminished influence of each individual citizen as the power and noise from organizations becomes all that can be heard, as they influence governments towards their own objectives. These organizations have proliferated in number, expanded in power, and unleashed their willingness to openly act to influence the government and the vote. They are much more willing than they were in the past to openly align their organization with a political party and ideology, often not directly related to their organization's primary mission, and to actively work to move the direction of voters and the nation. These organizations include corporations, public sector unions, private unions, the journalist media, widely varying single issue ideology groups, foreign governments, entertainment media, higher education, and transnational organizations, to name a few. Each competes to influence the choices of individual voters, and to influence representatives directly. It is correct to view representation as a zero-sum game: as the power or influence of organizations increases, the relative power of each voter is reduced. The effect is true even in cases where the citizen directly chooses the representative through the ballot and directly controls the actual vote but becomes convinced by the organization to believe their messages and views. If the organization did not exist or was less powerful, that voter may have made a different choice which better aligns to their own known interests. The powerful messaging sometimes overcomes both self-interest and good reason.

4. **The macro level changes in the world will continue** to bring increased competition and competition across different areas to

the next generation of Americans and across much of the world. It is imperative to the nation's future that the next generation is given the support to prepare for this new level of competition. The most fundamental and essential support comes from their family, and that family must be empowered with equal representation through the vote. These macro level changes include those that often fall under the broad term of globalization, but many others are related to technology innovations and social change.

The remainder of this chapter covers each of the four areas of change in greater detail.

1. National Demographic Changes

– Selective parenthood
In the not too distant past, like it or not, nearly all of adult society was directly involved with raising children or had strong connections to children through relatives, friends and neighbors. These connections created a greater understanding of their needs and concern for their wellbeing, and indirectly maintained some common prioritization of their issues. In a society with those relationships, one could trust that children were reasonably well represented by the distribution of votes among the entire adult population. Most adults were either parents, extended relatives, or in some way directly connected. That fact created a greater shared societal concern for the issues of children and young families.

Most adults directly interacted with minors on a very regular basis. Nuclear families were larger, composed of a higher number of children in each family, and extended families were consequently much larger due to the multiplier effect. Since the prior generation had more children, adults who did not have children of their own had connection to related children through their much larger extended family. In addition, a more agrarian and rural population with lower geographic mobility supported a longer period of connection to related children and to unrelated children in the surrounding neighborhood and local community.

The emergence of a large population of adults not connected to children, whether by choice, demographics, or by other factors, creates a very different environment for society and for the nation's future.

The population distribution of minors was very different for most of human civilization. In the United States, the first census of 1790 indicated that 50% of population was under age 16, compared to 22 % of the population now. The shift in population distribution is the result of changes in both the birth rate and through a dramatic increase in longevity. The reduction in the proportion of minors and their families within the general population will continue and the trend can make matters much worse. The birth rate has been declining steadily since the early 20th century. The baby boom following World War II partially disrupted the declining trend of the 20th century, but excluding that disruption, it has trended steadily downward and continues into the 21st century. The U.S. birth rate reached a 20th century peak of 3.7 lifetime births per woman in the late 1950's, well above the replace-ment rate of 2.1, and then began a decline which coincided with the improved quality and availability of birth control.[2] It continued to decline with the introduction of the first oral contraceptive in 1960. By the 1970's energy crisis and economic downturn, the U.S. fertility rate dipped to 1.74 in the bicentennial year of 1976. Continuing this trend, the 2018 fertility rate was the lowest on record since the government began tracking fertility rates at 1.73, and the lowest absolute number of births in 32 years.

Smaller nuclear and extended families are now the norm, so it is possible for many adult citizens to live most of adult life with little or no connection to children. In the 1790 census, 90% of the population lived in households of 4 people or greater.[3] By 1940 this dropped to two thirds or 66%; by 1980 it was 50%, and down to 43% in 2011 and continues to decline.[4]

These changes create a new political environment for our democracy. In this new reality, children are no longer represented by the current distribution of adult voters. As a result, their representation is becoming marginalized as one would expect for any disenfranchised group within a democracy.

To highlight the scale of this issue, a simple approach is to assess how the voting power currently distributes now, without representation, and compare it to what it would be with minors having representation as citizens of an authentic democracy, i.e., if a proxy vote was established. Based on U.S. census estimates for 2019, there are approximately 74M minors, with 67 M adult parents and guardians caring for them. That 67 M represents 27% of the adult population and therefore 27% of votes, with the remaining population of 181M adults comprising the other 73%. Some arithmetic shows over a 2 ½ to 1 advantage in voting power for adults who are not representing minors, despite the reality that those parents represent 43% of citizens - themselves and their children. Consider the implications for national priorities which most effect younger families. Although many of these areas - public education, managing federal debt, long term environmental issues, higher education, etc. - concern most citizens who are not parents, there is a very different level of concern when the issue has a very direct impact on your life, compared to an issue that is among many abstract tradeoffs for the nation. The belief that we have a fair democracy certainly comes into question when such a large portion of the population is systematically not represented. As you will note in the chapter that follows, the results of this gap are policy biases that negatively affect the underrepresented group.

– Longevity and the aging population

The broad advances in medical care have increased our longevity and the quality of life that we can anticipate in later years. Not only are we living longer, but we are living healthier lives and remaining more active and with a higher quality of life. All good! And we would expect that this should have a direct effect on society. In this context, the natural result of the higher longevity means greater proportion of older adults in the adult population, and therefore a much larger population that has either limited or no direct connection to child rearing and to children. Those over 50 increased from 26% of the adult population to 42% of the adult population between 1910 and 2018, nearly all of that the result of the growth coming from the 60+ group, which increased from 8% to 24% of the adult population. These are large increases in a politically powerful group. Not only is it a powerful group, but it is a group with a distinctly different set of needs from those of minors and a sometimes competing set of needs.

As a group, older Americans are not in in direct competition with minors. However, their core needs and concerns require substantial government resources, and their core needs are very different than those of minors, naturally causing them to influence major policy decisions in a way that can be quite different compared to the needs of minors. As important as the conflict of needs is the lack of direct connection to the needs and issues of minors. Without direct responsibility for minors and with many having minimal contact with minors, it is not reasonable to expect older Americans to be aware or prioritize the minor's needs compared with the many real and pressing concerns of citizens in their later years. (I hope this was stated carefully enough for the AARP and my fellow older Americans). Older Americans would therefore naturally have a bias to elect representatives who address their own known needs.

For a more concrete example, consider the choice between a politician who would like to raise taxes to improve the quality of local schools, and another who would focus on expanding Medicare coverage and reducing real estate taxes. A voter's preference may be highly influenced by that voter's stage in life and personal priorities during that life stage. An American might view the choice one way now, but that same American might choose differently 25 years later; for example, choosing the support of local schools during their child rearing years, and later be more concerned about Medicare and reducing taxes.

This older group will also continue to increase in size and power, expanding the longer term power imbalance with the families of minors. The minors become more marginalized as the voting power of the parents of minors continues to diminish in a relative comparison to older Americans.

Beyond the direct impact on political power through the vote, there are other important factors which shift the balance of power towards older Americans. First, there is a much higher likelihood that the over 50 have accumulated sufficient wealth to donate to political causes and to directly influence elections. For example, for the citizen population aged 30-39, the average of the top 10% of households has accumulated wealth of $370,000. Since many of the parents within this group aspire to sending their children to college or to help them launch their lives in another way, and are still building their own lives and careers, nearly all of this accumulated wealth is held closely and not disposable. For many it is planned for a specific future use and basic security. Consequently, it is not available for use in influencing political causes. In sharp contrast, for Americans over 55, that top 10% group has accumulated wealth of $1.5 Million, and the 55+ are either receiving or can anticipate a pension or Social Security in the near future. There is an enormous difference between these adults in their ability to donate to political causes and groups. It is impossible to measure how much money matters in influencing politics, but there is enough anecdotal evidence that there should be no requirement to prove that it does. It matters.

Another difficult to quantify, but equally important advantage of those over 55, is the greater social and political influence. This is developed over time through personal relationships throughout the many years that it takes to learn how to leverage influence and power. There is nothing sinister or unfair about this - it is inherent in the development of each individual. The point is simply that it has the natural effect of helping more experienced citizens move their issues up the priority stack, and therefore lowering the relative position of other groups' priorities. Beyond wealth and influence, those over 55 have more time; time to devote to civic and political activities. While a parent with minor children is struggling with a long task list to support their child's edu-cational and social development, along with managing their own devel-oping job or career, or simply paying bills, an older American may be free to choose to go to a political rally or support a candidate through political party activity or through issue centered initiatives. The Bureau of Labor Statistics indicates that between ages 25-44 (Bureau Of Labor Statistics, 2019)[5], the average person has 4.3 hours per day (including weekends) for leisure and civic activities, moving to 7.4 hours for over 55, or over 70% more free time. This doesn't seem to properly capture the time constraints of working parents, but it does give a small level of comparison.[6]

This lack of political power of minors and their families is a current problem. It will increase quickly as the size, wealth, and political power of the group of older Americans continues to grow relative to the rest of the population. Between 2019 and 2050, the over 65 group will grow from 16% to 22% of the overall population and will quickly overtake the size of the population of minors and of adults who represent minors.

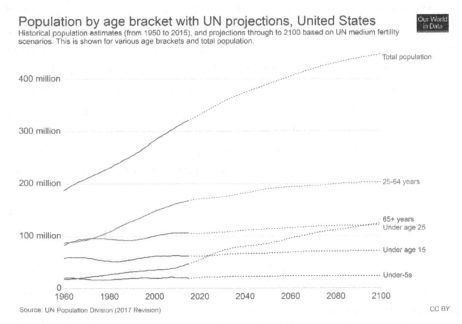

Population distribution of the United States by Age group[7]

–Geographic mobility

A third area that reduces the connectedness to children and therefore the ability of the general population of adults to represent children's needs, is the increase in geographic mobility. Increased geographic mobility, and the increase in the distance of that mobility, reduces the exposure of some of the population to the current issues of children and young families. Several factors combine to contribute to the high mobility rate of our population, at over 11% moving yearly; the vast geographic size of the US, the migration to the west and to the south, the emergence of planned retirement communities, and the recent shifts to return to urban areas. Mobility further reduces direct connections to minors for those who choose to be child-free and for older Americans to their young relatives. The natural result is the reduced prioritization of children's issues against competing priorities.

Combined, the continued decrease in birth rate, increase in the older population, and geographic mobility, further reduce the relative political power and voting representation of young families. With limited influence, we should expect their issues to receive lower priority, consequently increasing the cost and difficulty of raising children. This inevitably results in a vicious cycle of population decline in the future, further reducing the current below-replacement fertility rates now common among most developed nations.[1] There are no malevolent villains conspiring to create or orchestrate these factors; these are simply changes in society and in our world which push the priorities of minors and of young families down on the list of many competing priorities and concerns.

2. The Massive Growth in the Government

As federal, state and local governments and the judiciary have grown in power, they increasingly determine who wins and loses across many

---

1 Some citizens believe that reducing the size of the population by reducing the birth rate is a benefit. Chapter 4 will review the many negative consequences and argue that the negative aspects of a declining population far outweigh the benefits of decline.

aspects of the life of each citizen. The growth of the government and government power has not been linear with the growth of the nation and economy. It has far outstripped the level of our growth in population and in the growth of economic output. The most accessible measure compares government spending levels to the national output, which has grown from less than 3 % of national output in 1900 to 24 % in 2012. (Schuler, 2014) This is not just a phenomenon of federal government spending, but is growing similarly at the state and local levels. When interest on the debt is included, government spending had reached 43% of Gross Domestic Product by 2011.[8]

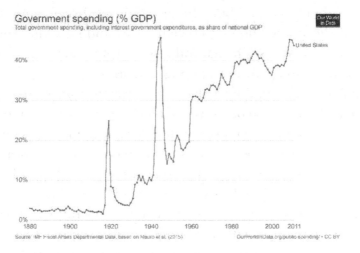

U.S. Government Spending as a percent of GDP
including interest on the Debt.[9]

The direct impact of government spending is only a one piece of the puzzle. Beyond gathering and redistributing economic resources, the government has also grown to establish laws and regulations and become more involved in all areas of citizens lives. A very recent example is the Affordable Care Act which established the framework for all health care insurance available to citizens and imposed a requirement to be covered. It extended health care to many who could not be covered due to preexisting conditions and reduced costs for some citizens enabling them to be covered. At the same time, it limited the ability for some citizens to access the physician of their choice, and lowered costs for some citizens by raising costs for others. The political parties and partisans will argue on its merits, but they all must agree that it moved the federal government firmly into health care decisions. Similarly, there is a constantly expanding set of laws, rules, and regulations that reach into many areas of life which previously would have been the free choice of citizens. Beyond these decisions from representative government, the judiciary has also become more assertive in compelling specific behaviors and reaches deeply into many aspects of public life, personal life, and commerce.

Government representatives, agencies, and the courts determine the winners and losers, in the economy, and in the direction of the culture. This increases the importance of government representation in each successive election cycle. That will continue. We can expect occasional efforts to modify the speed or even turn back the dial for a time, but the long-term trend is clear. The theses here is not to suggest a new method for government to be limited or dialed back, nor increased in influence, but simply to highlight that the stakes are high and growing, and therefore balanced representation becomes more important. This continued growing power of the government magnifies the importance that minors be represented. Without representation, they will continue to become marginalized simply through a lack of power, always lower on the priority stack than other groups.

3. Emergence of Powerful Organizations

Concentrated power has always been the enemy of liberty.

—Ronald Reagan

Our democracy does not exist in a vacuum where well informed citizens carefully and independently consider government policy decisions and then select representatives that align with their choices. Naturally, every citizen has limitations in gathering and assessing information; limited by their time, interest, and their ability to assess the information they receive and the implications of alternative policy choices. The information citizens receive cannot be magically filtered to be factual and unbiased, so a large component of the democratic process centers on communicating and influencing perceptions – of citizens, government representatives, and of government agencies.

As organizations continue to grow in power, their ability to influence the vote, and directly to influence representatives and government agencies increases, drowning out or modifying the individual citizen's perceived concerns. The effect on minors is that this shifts the priorities away from their interest in two ways – first, since most organizations are geared to the concerns and needs of older populations of constituents, they crowd out the issues of minors; second, organizations leaders are generally much older, as a natural consequence of what is needed to rise in an organization, creating another bias in the priorities of organizations. This section introduces the challenge of the increasing power of organizations to minors. For a review of specific organization types and their impact, see Appendix A.

The United States is a heterogeneous and dynamically changing nation with many interest groups vying to influence perceptions and ultimately decisions in a way that supports their priorities. Each group has a distinct mix of objectives and approaches to exercising influence and power. Each organization is attempting to optimize their environment for their own interest by influencing voters and influencing government representatives and government officials in ways that are best for their group. Most of the influence is legal and fits within a reasonable ethical structure; there also are many outliers willing to cross all ethical, moral and legal lines. The range of methods for legally achieving influence are broad, including direct messaging to all voters to build support; forming industry groups or political action committees; aligning members of a union to vote for their candidates; directly influencing elected representatives and regulatory officials, and on through an extensive list of other methods.

Since organizations are composed of citizens, it may appear that they are not competing with citizens. However, the competition is not coming from the direct votes of their members and employees as citizens, but rather the hidden actions and concentrated financial resources of the large organization which actively competes with individual voters. The goals and interests of each organization are often very different from those of the general population of citizens, though they likely align with some subset of citizens. The organization views the world through a lens which identifies their priorities as paramount, not among a set of tradeoffs as would individual citizens. In many cases an organization can concentrate powerful forces and shift the balance of power in an election or on a referendum in a way that is not necessarily good, and often bad, for the general population. There is often no equally powerful entity to pull against the large organization, and without that, the organization can have tremendous leverage in influencing a government representative, and more broadly influencing the vote of many representatives to establish broad national power, shifting the direction of an individual election and even changing public opinion.

The rise in the power of organizations reduces the relative power of every individual citizen, but the impact is more disproportional for minors and their families.

A simple way to see this is to follow the money. A central objective of most organizations is accumulating financial resources to support their growth and yield power over their environment. The financial objective may be met from the sale of a product or service, through taxes, through membership dues or through donation. Since wealth and disposable income is skewed heavily towards older citizens, and since more disposable income and wealth is available to childfree adults, organizations naturally have a bias towards serving the needs of these constituents. It is the organization's target audience and market, so the issues that the organizations promote are the issues of their constituents, all in support of their own growth and success. There are exceptions, like consumer products companies where the target market is serving young families or family oriented political interest groups; but across the nation as a whole, the target is an older and more childfree population.

The leadership of organizations also skews heavily to an older population, since it generally takes many years to rise through the ranks within the hierarchy. This natural effect creates a bias for the opinions and viewpoints of the older Americans making decisions at the executive level and at the Board of Directors level.

For most organizations that seek to influence social, regulatory and governmental issues, the most cost effective method for gaining influence over their environment is through directly influencing government officials and elected representatives. Although paying a representative directly is considered a bribe and clearly illegal, donating repeatedly to a political party, or to an elected official's political campaign, or foundation, or through a single issue political organization is perfectly legal. There are many different and clever ways to influence regulatory officials which can also be quite effective and remain legal.

It is impossible to track all funds related to this purchase of influence, but some of these are more visible since they must be declared. These can help to place a sense of context and scale on the value of influencing government decisions and give a sense of proportion of their impact. One area of spending that must be declared is the spending on official lobby groups. In 2016, the declared amounts included in lobbying firm data for 2016 included over 11,000 lobbyists, the equivalent of 21 lobbyists per member of Congress; with $3.1 Billion declared as spent on lobbying, or $6 Million per member of Congress; the equivalent of more than $10 per U.S. citizen. That level of spending has been relatively stable since 2008, at that time at 14,000 lobbyists and $3.3 Billion in spending. (Open Secrets.Org, 2019)[10] These figures surely understate the full spending level. The reduction in the number lobbyists between 2008 and 2016, was not due to less lobbying, but reflects the practice of more professionals in the field rebranding themselves as something other than lobbyists - as advisors or using other terms that avoids a technical classification as a lobbyist. Similarly, the spending is likely understated since the spending aligns to the professionals who have rebranded away from being classified as lobbyists.

Lobbyist organizations and the groups designated for lobbying within other large organizations are only a small piece of the financial puzzle. Many other organizations, individuals, and nations actively seek to modify our nation's decisions and direction to their advantage; most to the advantage of the group they represent, with a few towards what the individuals within the group personally believe. The 2016 election provides an example of the extent of financial flows from the lobbyists, bundlers, and other organizations. In 2016, a total of $3.6 Billion was spent across the two major parties, or $28 per citizen that voted. (OpenSecrets.Org, 2019)[11] The total presidential election portion of the spending, including donations from citizens was $1.2B spent for the two leading parties, or over $9 per vote.

For some organizations, there is a broad strategic alignment with a political party. The declared political party alignment of U.S. citizens is split nearly evenly between Democrat, Republican and Independent. In nearly all elections, voters are choosing between the two leading parties. With that even balance of voters, the choice of large organizations to align with a political party can be in conflict with a significant portion of end customers, constituents, employees, or partners. The organization's leaders determine that the alignment to meet certain objectives justifies accepting this conflict or contradiction. This can lead to any citizen's indirectly or directly financing an organization in conflict with their own personal interests and beliefs. For public companies, it can mean influencing an election in conflict with the preferences of the corporation's shareholders, effectively its owners.

Unfortunately, this, along with some of the sleazy practices of influence peddling gets relatively little attention, although it is deeply understood by much of our population and creates some cynicism among many voters who note the obvious and frequent conflicts. The large amount of money and power at stake in these policy decisions attracts powerful forces that undermine the democratic process towards their own ends.

So how does the growth in power of these organizations effect the representation of minors?
These groups compete for mindshare of all voters and their representatives on the issues important to the groups. While their influence may align with the interests of some citizens, most organizations do not reflect the general public, but rather they are a subset of the group pulling towards their preferred direction. Many of these organizations actively work to focus the nation's attention on their priorities and attempt to shift the dialogue in their favor, usually inflating the importance of their chosen issue among their target voters.

Unfortunately, these organizations continue to grow more powerful and effective relative to the power of an individual citizen. Naturally their activities are driven by their own interests. More recently they have become less reticent about broadcasting their active presence and their political influence, something that was previously done more quietly. The relative alignment with the needs of young families varies by organization across a broad spectrum, ranging from well-aligned and correlated, to uncorrelated and unrelated, to directly conflicting. The groups represent a powerful force and an important part of the economy and society, but they effectively cut-in-line in priority for their interests over those of young families in a resource limited environment. Like any other cutting in line, their prioritization of self seems justified to the group themselves, but the result is simply the powerful winning priority, and the least powerful and least aggressive groups getting de-prioritized to the back of the line. Like in kindergarten.

We have the best government that money can buy.

—MARK TWAIN

Appendix A examines several categories of organizations and their impact.

This discussion does not suggest that we create additional constraints upon free speech, nor upon the ability of organizations to actively lobby representatives to best achieve their objectives. Instituting constraints would likely require changes in free speech protections and bring a new larger set of problems. This only seeks to highlight the power of large organizations to further marginalize the influence of minors and their families. The nation must restore a better balance by implementing a proxy vote for minors.

4. The Macro Level Change in the World

"It is not the strongest of the species that survive, nor the most intelligent, but the one most responsive to change."

—Charles Darwin

The fourth major category of reasons that the U.S. must establish representation for minors are the macro level changes which further shifts the field of global competition towards competing on the basis of knowledge and collaborative skills. If this trend continues, the nations that will succeed are the ones willing to commit to substantially invest in the development of their education systems and methods. The proxy vote will create the shift in focus of the nation's representatives to make the investment.

Several macro level changes are already underway which will bring increasing competition to the next generation. Globalization overlays many of the changes and has increased the competition of future U.S. citizens with their peers throughout the world. They will compete on many dimensions – through the competition of their companies, through competition in education, science, innovation, and in the geopolitical competition between nations. In each dimension there will continue to be dynamic change, with winners largely decided by the ability to adapt to the new changes and to adopt new skills and methods.

The pace of change and the acceleration in the pace of change has been underway for some time and we should anticipate that the future path will continue in this way. It is difficult to have an accurate perspective on the pace of change in the world simply through our daily experience. Perceiving the cadence and dynamism requires substantial thought - thinking back over a period of time and reflecting on the change. The unpredictable nature of the change is equally difficult to perceive, since that requires remembering and considering past expectations, and comparing to what actually did happen during the period. For any longer period of time, that would require a more detailed future forecast and better recall then most can honestly claim. Forecasting how the exogenous factors like technology change, world politics, cultural values changes, etc., will affect our lives over a long period is simply not where we apply most think time. Most of life doesn't require that kind of forethought, which is good because the lack of predictability would make most of it a wasted exercise in forecasting. Life is experienced in real time and insightful perspective about global factors requires too much knowledge and time for analysis and deep reflection. It is normal for most of us to be sufficiently busy with managing daily life, so we tend to reflect with shorter term time horizons.

Let's pause to do that for a moment to make this point more clear, and then return to implications for the proxy. Think back to your own life 30 years ago if you are old enough, or if you are not, try to consider someone else's life at that time. Over the last 30 years, since 1989, most aspects of our lives have changed in ways that we could never have predicted. The political environment of the world was very different and more immediately threatening. In 1989, the USSR was 2 years from dissolving, and we were 40 years into a tense nuclear-armed Cold War. The Warsaw Pact of communist nations was intact, with all those nations aligned with the USSR and positioned in opposition to the western nations and were still 4 years from dissolving into independent nations. The violent suppression at China's Tiananmen Square was still a year away and the nation was about to experience a revival of Maoist Ideology. The U.S. commercial relationships with China were just beginning. The U.S. public was still highly concerned about its ability to compete economically with Japan, which was demonstrating excellence and leadership in automobiles and electronics.

In technology, fifteen percent of Americans had access to a personal computer at home, with three percent having something resembling an internet connection and virtually no public email and one tenth of one percent of the population had a mobile phone. Personal Digital Assistants had not been conceived yet, which later combined with mobile phones into Smartphones. The rest of the world was at an even earlier stage of personal technology adoption.

The world was beginning to move to a more fully integrated global economy, with international trade just beginning a steady increase. Over the next 25 years, from 1987 to 2011, the pace of world trade growth increased dramatically, moving up another 25% to 59% of world GDP. (Robert C. Feenstra, 2015)[12] At the same time and largely a consequential result, from 1987 to 2015, worldwide extreme poverty dropped by 1.2 Billion from 1.9 Billion to 0.7 Billion people, at the same time that global population increased from 5.0 B to 7.3 Billion, or from 24% to less than 10% of the population. There are many good things that have happened in the world over the past 30 years, and there is reason to believe that we will continue to see improvements in the next 30 years.

This level of dynamic change heightens the importance of establishing the proxy vote. Global competition between societies has already reached a high level, high enough for us to understand that many of our industries compete directly with companies across a very large world. Though some industries are insulated due to a physical proximity advantage, (hospitals, retail, finance), others have no such protection and experience extensive competition (autos, other manufacturing, agriculture, etc.). The competition is not only at the broad level of industry but has begun to now include competition at the level of workers and citizens. In many industries, low cost workers in other countries can offer a competitive cost advantage. Firms can use outsourcing to distribute segments of the value chain of a business into physically dispersed locations. Firms in the U.S. can move some activities to other locations for financial, portfolio or political reasons, or simply recruit lower cost personnel from other countries, and foreign graduates of U.S. universities to gain a financial edge.

The future is uncertain, but one area that seems easy to forecast with certainty is that U.S. citizen employees will be increasingly in competition with employees from other nations as communications and physical proximity barriers continue to decline. It is not possible to prevent that competition, but there are ways to improve our competitive position. The first and most important step to help minor citizens in the U.S. prepare for this competition, is by providing the proxy vote to their families, bringing the political power to the decision makers (their parents), who can use this to focus the attention of government representatives on the need to prepare.

Global Competition

The Competitive Advantage of Nations, published in 1990 by Harvard Professor Michael Porter, offers the first comprehensive theory of competitiveness at the national level, moving beyond the view that a nation's advantages are based primarily on natural resources and labor productivity. Professor Porter introduces a diamond framework to describe the interrelationship between four key factors that determine the national environment within which corporations compete: 1) Factor conditions – the position in the factors of production, namely raw materials, energy, qualified employees, etc.; 2) Demand conditions – the nature of home market demand for a market. 3) Supplier and partner industry presence; 4) Firm Strategy, Structure and Rivalry – which are the conditions within the nation which allow firms to be formed and managed and the rules which govern competition. The basic concepts are used in the following discussion.

There are several sources of competitive advantage which supported the continuous growth of the United States. The expansion from small colonial towns and farms totaling 1 million people in 1700 to one of the world's leading powers was not a single random event, good fortune, excellent planning, or the results of having the population with the purest virtue, but rather the combination of many important contributing factors. Some were natural factor advantages, like the physical advantage of plentiful arable land with relatively mild climate, extensive natural resources, and physical separation from other large nations resulting in fewer early wars. Many of the US's competitive advantages were the results of quite a few hard-fought and wise choices of early settlers and the Founding Fathers and Mothers, establishing a competitive market economy structure, shared values which reject historic hierarchical government management schemes (though their adjustments were certainly incomplete and imperfect), fostering broader participation in self-government, a higher openness to immigration attracting many new immigrants who came with a driving commitment to improve their lives, and a belief that improvement could happen. The decision to preserve the union and outlaw slavery was extremely costly in lives but was important for how the nation and world have progressed. There was an early commitment to public education, then compulsory education and higher education, early adoption of new manufacturing and farming technologies, then continuing through other technologies including railroads, cars, electrical, electronic, computer, scientific, medicines, etc. So many important decisions, and so many related to maximizing the potential of each individual and leveraging natural resources and innovation enabling each individual to become more efficient and effective.

Beyond these advantages, for much of the 20th century the U.S. held a comparative advantage vs. much of the world partially as a result of the devastation and loss of productive capacity of many nations through cataclysmic World Wars. Much of Western European manufacturing was devastated after WWII, and the Soviet Union and Warsaw bloc nations were reeling and also under the new cloud of communist repression, self-inflicted famine and genocide, along with slow growth and no innovation. The colonial empires were unravelling, and the colonies were demanding and fighting for freedom and in early stages of building basic independent economies. From 1945 to 1965, the U.S. was preeminent, while the rest of the world continued to rebuild.

Over the last 50 years, many nations of the world have surged forward to improve the quality of life of their citizens, partly by improving their national competitive positions. The improvements are broad and include supporting enablers like strategic trade agreements EEOC, NAFTA, or simply establishing deeper new trading with the U.S. as in Korea, China and Vietnam. Some nations created competitive advantage through strategic investment like Taiwan's investments in semiconductor manufacturing, Japan's in autos and electronics, South Korea's in electronics. Others have improved their advantage through control of resources, like OPEC, Russia, and Venezuela. Others sought advantage through investments in literacy, education and business friendly regulation like Singapore, which has made world leading improvements effecting all areas of business competitiveness. The U.S. still has many sources of advantage, but it now has many competitors, unlike that advantaged starting point immediately following WWII.

The generations of Americans that will determine America's future continue to change with each era. Almost gone is the "Great Generation", forged in steel, living through the daily survival challenges of the Great Depression followed by the survival challenges of World War II. Beyond personal survival, they lived with the prospect of a very uncertain future, so that even survival may be in a bleak world of long-term poverty or repression, in a world split between different forms of fascist and communist dictators.

The generations which followed, often referred to as the Silent Generation and then the Baby Boomers inherited a world that was better, but not idyllic, with 40+ years of the Cold War, the threat of nuclear war, hard fought battles for equality and civil rights, McCarthy era injustice, etc. They inherited the benefits of a nation with a clear competitive advantage throughout that time, since most of the world was struggling to recover. Many other parts of the world were in far worse situations than simple economic recovery, fighting for basic freedom from colonialism, or suffering under communist or other dictatorships. Many dictatorships were still struggling with their opposition, using mass killings to exterminate potential dissent, and many experimenting with failed economic policies, driving their nations into mass poverty and famine – (see Stalin, Mao, the Khmer Rouge, North Korea's Kim Il Sung, Mengistu Haile Mariam in Ethiopia).

The turmoil of that world continues, with tragic loss of life, privation, and disruption in Syria, Venezuela, North Korea, Nigeria, Somalia, South Sudan and Yemen. But the largest among the world's non-democratic nations have begun to learn how to use trade and the free market system to begin to compete, and many have sufficiently crushed internal dissent to allow them to move beyond their internal struggles to compete globally. Their leaders are now learning to use technology to monitor and control their populations. They are now also actively seeking to use our open political system against us, and use other stealthy methods to support their aims, like cyber warfare, unfair trade practices that steal technology, spying, tampering with elections and supporting international turmoil. We compete with them now, both economically and politically. We also compete with our allies economically in Europe and Asia, with many nations and large populations with free, ambitious citizens who share similar values to ours. We all share the same genetic material and aspirations for a better life. We must therefore recognize that all of these are worthy competitors, both friends and foes - we will be competing with all of them in the future.

The next generation of Americans must be prepared to compete in this increasingly global environment and do so with the perspective of a wise competitor after a win – with respect and appreciation of the competitor's skills and determination. That is the opposite of entitlement and the belief that our success will come naturally, so we can go on vacation, entertain ourselves and retire early to leave the work to others. Instead, like any competitor who wants to remain successful over the long term, the U.S. must not underestimate its competition on any dimension. That level of commitment always comes through a decision to take the competitive environment seriously and to be rigorous in committing to take the additional steps necessary to be successful. Assume that the competitor will do so, therefore the next generation of Americans must be prepared for the same.

This level of global competition will continue to increase. Competitive barriers are continuing to be reduced, and proximity barriers are being removed through instantaneous communications, transportation reliability and safety, continuously rising education levels, more demanding consumers, a reduction in the danger of interruption due to war, and the need for combinations of skills and technologies to deliver advanced products. These all conspire to make our economies more interrelated and more openly competitive. Every nation will face the tradeoff between applying resources to adjust to global competition vs. attempting to protect internal industries from external markets; the answer is not always clear.

The nature of future competition
The heightened level of competition across the globe from the late 19th to 21st centuries is correlated to the large growth in population, combined with the introduction of an enormous number of new technologies, especially in communications and transportation technologies which reduce the longstanding barriers of distance and information transfer in the competition between nations.

As other barriers continue to lower, it is the needs and capabilities of all the world's people which determine the factors of competition that become the most central to success. As the nature of competition continues to change, the societies that succeed are those that adapt to the new conditions and demands. For example, having control of abundant arable land was once the most important source of economic competitive advantage. With much of the population living near subsistence, the ability to feed your population and your armies was central to growing your population to sufficient scale for defense or expansion. Food products could also provide a desired commodity for trade. Maintaining or expanding control over arable land vs. potential competitors was also important, so military technology was important. The relative size of population vs. the size of competitors was important. This allowed control of more arable land, growing population resources by converting the invaded peoples into slaves, workers, soldiers, or tribute payers, and stealing their goods for disposal. These realities of competition created a very hostile world for thousands of years.

It was not until the early 18th century that innovations in farming techniques and machines began to significantly break the longstanding yield limitations on arable land, making it much more productive, and reducing the competitive value of arable land. Another example of a source of advantage was the development of unique and desired goods, from raw materials like copper, gold, silver, etc. to items that others wanted, like tools, silk, glass, metal, etc. Eventually the demand and commerce in these led to technology innovations across metallurgy, mining and manufacturing.

Another example of a source of competitive advantage is geographic location and its impact on commerce. For over a thousand years prior to the 15th century, the Byzantine Empire, the Ottoman Empire, and later Venice, each depended on their physical position as a primary source of competitive advantage for trade between the Far East and Europe on the "Silk Road" and the "Spice Route". The desire to bypass these areas led to Christopher Columbus's accidental landing on the North American continent. This location advantage was displaced by the emergence of shipping routes as a result of the Age of Discovery, with Portugal, England, Holland, and Spain, each introducing shipping to displace the location advantage of a central geographic position for commerce. This change in location advantage led to the eventual decline of Venice's great wealth and economic power and was an important factor in the later decline of the Ottoman Empire. These simple and accessible examples of past sources of national competitive advantage serve as a reminder that the field of competition among societies can move from one arena to another and that change has existential results for the societies.

The 20th century witnessed changes in the dimensions of competition along with vast geopolitical changes globally in every corner of the world, with a clear acceleration of change compared to the prior century. The 20th century changes included the dissolution of established Empires and colonial powers, e.g. the Russian Empire to the Union of Soviet Socialist Republics (USSR), to simply the nation of Russia and many independent republics; the dissolution of the British, French, German, Japanese Empires, the rise of the Communist dictatorship as a successful new model of repression and dominance by a small oligarchy in places like Cuba and Venezuela, and the dissolution and fragmentation of the former Ottoman Empire into Turkey and several unstable middle-eastern states. The world is also incomparably wealthier, with much lower poverty, much higher literacy (moving from 21% to 85% worldwide), far fewer war deaths, longer life expectancies, and a more connected population with technology that was unimaginable 100 years ago. We cannot know what is ahead, but there is every reason to believe that the 21st century will experience at least the same pace of change or continuing the trend to an even faster pace of change.

We know that the nature of competition will continue to change. The level, speed, and the most impactful areas of change are uncertain, but the general theme and categories of change is more apparent. For this discussion, we'll focus on economic competition, which is currently a large component of the overall competition among nations.

What is past is prologue.

—**WILLIAM SHAKESPEARE**

Let's look back on the past for a moment to provide perspective on the possible future. The past roughly 60 years is often characterized as the Information Age or the Era of the Digital Revolution. These terms have high flexibility in how they are used, sometimes referring to the revolution within the electronics industry and the industry's products, moving from analog to digital circuitry, to the much more broad definition which captures the related changes across all industries and consumer uses. The broadest meaning of the Digital Revolution includes the full range of innovation that digital technology and computing have enabled, as well as the effects on other industries, consumer's lives, and society. The core of this is the circuitry and logic of processors, communication protocols, storage technologies, semiconductor design and manufacturing processes, followed by networking, internet, mobile technology, digital information storage, digital media, light-emitting diodes (LED's), to additional product groups like smartphones, cloud computing, Apps and user software, Email, ecommerce and social networking, bar codes scanners, ATM's. Yes, quite a lot of underlying technologies, each with their own components and software. Continuing further afield to changes in other fields which are enabled directly by digital technology, e.g. human genome mapping, DNA sequencing, DNA testing, Magnetic Resonance Imaging (MRI), GPS systems, Digital photography/videography, laparoscopy (arthroscopic surgery), photovoltaic cells (solar energy), radio frequency identification (RFID) and applications (e.g. EZ Pass), many life science and drug development uses.[13]

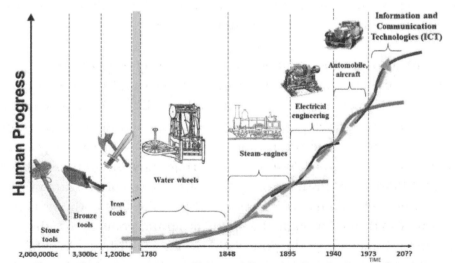

Source: Hilbert and Cairo, 2008; Cristopher Freeman et al. *As time goes by*, 2001. Schumpeter, (1939). *Business Cycles: A Theoretical, Hist., & Stat. Analysis of the Capitalist Process.*

It is not clear if the world is approaching a new era that is the result of a breakthrough that is still unrecognized, (by definition), but there is enough known about the current technologies that are in development, to support the belief that the innovations of the Digital Revolution can continue for at least the next 25 years. The proliferation of technology into many industries and disciplines should continue, while at the same time we already know that there will be continued improvements in the areas already underway - most clearly through continued increases in processing power, portability, lower power use, and increasing software development improvements. We've experienced at least fifty years of continuous innovation and the future can continue to build upon the momentum of this Digital Revolution.

Some of the future categories of innovation have already begun to make headway with investment and with purchases by early adopters, like IOT (Internet of Things which includes smart grid, home automation/smart homes, virtual power plant, building automation, health monitoring, etc.), autonomous vehicles, robotics, blockchain technology, virtual reality, augmented reality, biometric technologies, machine learning, biotechnologies and bioinformatics across agriculture, food production, and medicine, genetic mapping and engineering etc. Yes, this long explanation and list is for a reason – as a reminder of what it means to prepare the next generation to compete.

So what does this tell us about change in the nature of competition?
The expansion of digital technologies into new and different arenas creates new opportunities to innovate and establish leadership in many new branches of development, and the contrary, to lose the leadership where we have it. The future opportunity is less tethered to innovation within the United States than during early innovations in the Digital Revolution. In that early phase of this era, core research from corporate R&D labs like Bell Labs and IBM, cultivated in the years following WWII and through the space program, combined with U.S. economic leadership of the post-WWII world, established leadership in

many engineering and science related disciplines. Superior university research and education gave the U.S. an advantage. This reinforced the emergence of many technology centers which grew into powerful and focused ecosystems within certain categories of technology, and continues in Silicon Valley, Seattle, NY/NJ metro corridor, Portland, Austin, Boulder, Research Triangle/Raleigh, and Atlanta. But the old proximity advantage of being close to where the underlying hardware and software is developed has become nearly irrelevant since communications have improved to allow engineers in the other nations a greater ability to compete than they had in the past. Competing ecosystems have emerged in other nations, with many national governments recognizing the importance and value of winning and are therefore willing to provide support. Although the U.S. remains in a strong position to lead as the technologies proliferate and enter new areas, it will face a much higher level of competition from other nations and from foreign corporations.

Therefore, the U.S. must begin to view the future competitive environment and the nature of competition in a new way - not assuming what was in the past will continue in the future; nor with the naiveté that the nation can rely on some kind of mystically entitled advantage. This doesn't suggest fearing inevitable decline or imply uncontrolled catastrophe; nor encouraging protectionist barriers to attempt to stem the tide of change. Rather to approach the future with a realistic assessment of the variability and uncertainty of that future. In particular, focusing in areas where there is flexibility to prepare and adjust for what may come.

The United States will retain a natural resources advantage and some location advantage, both of which remain important. The physical location of North America still places great distance from enemies who might significantly threaten the nation in a direct war (non-nuclear), allowing greater security to potential investors than other nations, as does a relatively stable political environment and legal system, open markets, and a growing democracy. All of these reduce the cost of capital and attract continued outside investment. The vast magnitude and breadth of natural resources in the U.S. provide a lower cost and secure supply. These are important advantages.

In the near term, the U.S. also holds an advantage among leading institutions of higher education, particularly in STEM (science, technology, engineering and math) disciplines. Also significant is a language advantage, since much of the world translates important STEM research and documents into English. STEM education is important, but the specific technical skills and the problem solving techniques that they teach are not sufficient. The skills sought by many leading firms today move far beyond these to broader critical thinking, creativity, skills in working under ambiguity, solving complex problems, collaboration, working within teams, and leadership skills. Nearly all of these are learned skills, which can be developed during primary and secondary education, and advanced through higher education.

The central point of this is that the nature of the competition will change, and that the skills and readiness of citizens will be the key determining factor of who succeeds. Whether the U.S. is able to adjust its education systems quickly enough to address this for the next generation depends fully upon the power of the proxy vote to help influence government and our society to make that investment happen.

Increase in speed of change and innovation
Not only is the nature of competition changing, but the speed of change and innovation is increasing, compounding the need for the education and preparation of young citizens to become an effective workforce. This increase is happening across nearly all major industries in pursuit of performance improvements in methods, processes and business models. The same factors which have increased the level of global competition, i.e. larger global population, higher worldwide literacy rates, communications advances, distributed computing power, and the rise in global wealth, bringing more individuals into the processes of research, development, and innovation – all combine to increase the

speed of innovation and the speed of change. With the business models of every business experiencing continuous change and transformation, the flexibility and capabilities of the workforce will be central to the success of the businesses and societies, and to each individual in that workforce.

The World Economic Forum's annual review in 2016, *Employment, Skills and Workforce Strategy for the Fourth Industrial Revolution,* offers a clear call to action on skills development, "During previous industrial revolutions, it often took decades to build the training systems and labor market institutions needed to develop major new skill sets on a large scale. Given the upcoming pace and scale of disruption brought about by the Fourth Industrial Revolution, however, this is simply not an option. Without targeted action today to manage the near-term transition and build a workforce with futureproof skills, governments will have to cope with ever-growing unemployment and inequality, and businesses with a shrinking consumer base. Moreover, these efforts are necessary not just to mitigate the risks of the profound shifts underway but also to capitalize on the opportunities presented by the Fourth Industrial Revolution. The talent to manage, shape and lead the changes underway will be in short supply unless we take action today to develop it."[14] (World Economic Forum, 2016)

Many highly qualified and dedicated experts are working on education initiatives privately, through the public sector, through universities, and through work with foundations, and there are many success stories throughout the nation. But the level of change that is necessary on a national scale are beyond the reach of these worthy efforts. The proxy vote would provide the necessary political power to begin to make the broader changes necessary to encourage and energize the best of these and to make the foundational changes that are needed. The proxy vote provides the straightest and most assured path to proper investment and management of our education systems in the interest of the whole nation. Without that additional political power, it is almost a certainty that the embedded interests will continue to prevent the kinds of transformational change to our teaching and training systems, and we will be unable to achieve the commitment for the additional investment necessary to make these bold changes.

We cannot always build the future for our youth,
but we can build our youth for the future.

—Franklin D. Roosevelt

CHAPTER 2

Policy Bias Due to Lack of Representation

———

THE LAST CHAPTER DISCUSSED THE macro level changes which make it necessary to ensure that the interests of minor citizens are represented through a proxy vote. This chapter discusses the many areas where government decisions create a substantial and unjust disadvantage for minors and their families. In many of these areas, resolving the lack of representation of minors would quickly shift future government decisions and possibly the direction of American culture, improving the lives and futures of today's minors and future generations of Americans. For most western democratic republics the same issues exist and many are already suffering from the same problems for the next generation. This discussion focuses solely on the United States. The following is an outline of the areas where the lack of representation results in bias against minors and their families. Each area will be covered in this chapter:

   I)   Government spending
        1)   National debt
        2)   Social Security
        3)   Medicare
        4)   Unfunded pension liabilities
        5)   Healthcare and the Affordable Care Act
        6)   Tax policy

I Government Spending

1) The national debt – Achieving a reasonable level of understanding of the National Debt is not easy. The mental process of trying to actively consider its impact is daunting, confusing, and for many, can be frightening. Despite this, it is a valuable exercise for any citizen who would like to be well informed about American policy choices and government representation. By the middle of 2019, the U.S. National Debt had ballooned to $22.5 Trillion Dollars, or over $68,500 per citizen and rising. Yes, that was $68,500 per citizen, not $68,500 per family, nor is it $68,500 per taxpayer. Those citizens include adults and minors. When the next American citizen is born, our gift to them, along with the hospital bill to their parents, is the liability for the national debt and the yearly interest payments.[15] This fact, standing alone, is sufficient reason for minors and their families to be better represented in future government decisions. Simply put, from the pre-revolutionary war slogan: No taxation without representation.

In 2015 the level of National Debt increased to above the nation's Gross Domestic Product, essentially higher than the all the goods and services produced by the nation that year. The last time the nation crossed that line was in 1947, at the end of WWII and the beginning of the Cold War. In 2019, the debt level is anticipated to be 6% above Gross Domestic Product or $21.3 Trillion. Another measure that provides the sense of scale is the level of debt **per taxpayer** of $185,000. The size of these numbers makes them difficult for most citizens to conceptualize; like trying to perceive the scale of the universe or conceptualize infinity, or the miniscule level of nanoscale semiconductor components or molecules. But to have a reasonable perspective and context for any decision, a sense of proportion is essential. For perspective on national policy a conscientious citizen needs this sense of proportion. This human scale comparison seems missed by many of the nation's representatives who make decisions every year to grow the national debt with no end in sight.

Whether or not this is the right level of debt for the nation, or whether the decision about the level of debt is correct, or how the increase in borrowing will be used, these decisions affect the future of minors. Therefore, they should be represented in that taxation decision, since debt increases can fairly be viewed as taxation that will happen in the future, with the spending occurring now.

Let's take a brief detour to create more context before returning to the impact on unrepresented minors.

What is the right level of National Debt?
There is no consensus answer to this question. Just as for a household, the answer is a function of many factors. To simplify the issue, let's use an example at the family level. For a family with an income of $60,000 per year, mortgage debt of $160,000 on a home worth $200,000 might be completely reasonable and could be considered a sound investment decision. On the other hand, taking on $160,000 of credit card debt to buy luxury brand clothing, vacations, and video games would be considered too much debt and not a good investment. So, debt taken for the purchase of an underlying asset with stable value can be good, while debt taken for discretionary expenses is not so good, and not an investment. For a very different family, $1 Million of miscellaneous debt may

be fine for a family with $10 Million in assets and a $1 Million a year income. So income and the value of offsetting assets are also important for answering the question about the acceptable level of debt.

A different example is the perspective of a medical student who may seek debt to support themselves through the long process of education, internship and residency. The orthopedic surgical intern who required $250,000 in debt and many years of education and now making only $50,000 per year as an intern, may still have taken on an acceptable level of debt because of the prospect of earning $400K per year as an orthopedic surgeon. So even debt and income don't tell the full story, since it is not current income, but prospect of future income that can determine whether debt is reasonable. On the other hand, students who take on $50,000 in debt to receive a college degree that doesn't improve their financial prospects, may be making a fine personal choice for expanding their viewpoints in a way that improves the quality of their lives, but a poor and costly financial decision.

For the medical student with superior long-term prospects, the debt should appear a bit less threatening, though it may still be disturbing. If that same story was for a gambler, who believed they could make $400,000 income, by investing $250,000 at the poker table, most reasonable people would believe it to be a bad investment. The relative risk that the income will happen is equally important.

These examples demonstrate that the debt needs to be compared to overall assets, net worth and prospects for future income and the riskiness or relative certainty of that future income. Debt which is taken on to buy an asset which will appreciate, like a mortgage to buy a home or investment property, is very different than debt that is taken to live a profligate lifestyle or to simply not feel constrained in making normal and necessary lifestyle tradeoffs.

Household assets in the U.S. in 2019 were estimated at over $115 Trillion, corporate assets over $26 Trillion and Small Businesses over $13 Trillion. There is a great deal of wealth in the US, even compared to the U.S. National Debt. In addition, the United States directly owns valuable assets including 640 Million Acres of land, 28% of the nation's total surface area (Jacobs, 2010)[16], and mineral rights on and offshore that cover 2.5 Million Acres (Institute for Energy Research, 2013),[17] which one energy think tank, the Institute of Energy Research estimates at $128 Trillion in resources; a portion of those resources could accrue to the government if it chose to approve extraction through leasing rights. There are many, many other assets including buildings, dams, roads, military equipment, and leases, along with a long list of other valuable assets.

The exact value of the government's balance sheet is not calculated, and it would require extensive effort to do so, though it may be a worthwhile future endeavor, since it is essential for every business and many households. For this discussion, it is enough to recognize that there is healthy support and evidence to support the belief that the current level of debt is not yet excessive with respect to national assets. The most obvious sign of this is the high U.S. bond rating and the nation's ability to continue to finance its debt without having to resort to excessive interest and without a need to create inflation to diminish the value of the debt. Another supporting indicator is the continuing desire by foreign investors to invest in the United States by buying stocks and real estate; both are valued as a source of solid returns with a sense of lower risk compared to other investment options based on the nation's financial and political stability.

If the debt is not so frightening, why did we wade into this topic?

Despite the evidence that the nation can support the debt that has already accumulated, the vast size of the debt and the unwillingness of the nation's leaders to act decisively and cooperatively to limit its growth or to identify a sensible benchmark of acceptable growth, creates a major risk for minors and their families. In 2019, the Federal Budget passed with a relatively high level of bipartisan support. The Omnibus passed 300-128 in the House, and 83-16 in the Senate, with the Federal Budget deficit approaching $1 Trillion. So it's clear enough that the nation's current representatives as a whole believe that the debt level is not yet too high.

Many households, companies, and nations learn the hard way that debt can appear quite sustainable and fine for an extended period, right up to the moment that it is not. Once over that cliff, it becomes a catastrophe and it is not possible to recover without great suffering and drastic measures. More often than not, there is no extraordinary warning when the limit is about to be reached, just the same level of warning we receive every day about threats to our future. The entire nation learned this the hard way in 2008 during the housing crisis, as many other nations have learned for different reasons in the past and continue to learn every year.

Minors must be represented in decisions regarding how and why the nation's debt level is grown and managed. Without representation, the decision to increase debt will be skewed to allowing the debt to build and be increased and passed from one generation to the next – an intergenerational game of hot potato – until the game is over. Minors and their families will have a longer-term perspective than the average voter, with more 'skin in the game' in the growth of debt. They are more likely to require representatives to actively and demonstrably manage the tradeoffs in government spending and taxes, and to actively develop and explain why certain debt level targets are acceptable.

Adding a proxy for minors will not by itself solve the problem of the national debt, but since minors are the citizen group that will inevitably be responsible for carrying that debt, their voice should be included in future decisions. Then the decisions to continue to increase the debt can authentically be considered a decision made "by the people." Each newborn citizen is greeted at birth with responsibility for their share of $ 68,500 in debt and the accompanying interest payments; it's only fair that we allow their representatives to influence how future spending will be managed and to what extent that debt will continue to grow. That would be authentic representative democracy.

2) Social Security – and Medicare/Medicaid have grown to levels that make other federal government line items appear small by comparison. In 2019, Social Security spending will be just short of $1.05 Trillion. Since the huge scale of trillions are hard to grasp or remember, it's useful to bring these to the human scale of citizens. If every citizen were to pay an equal share annually to support these programs, each citizen - including minors, retired persons, the disabled, the unemployed, etc. – every citizen - would need to pay $3500 annually. That is every individual citizen, so for a family of four that total is almost $14K per year. This is just social security, so add another $700 Billion and $600 Billion for Medicare and Medicaid for the three largest areas of spending of the government. The next largest budget item is Defense spending which includes all spending for military personnel, facilities and equipment. That cost is projected to be $0.65 Trillion in 2019, or $2150 per citizen or roughly 28% of the combined spending on Social Security and Medicare/Medicaid.

Social Security and Medicare/Medicaid programs are unrivaled as the largest U.S. government managed programs to redistribute wealth, redistributing not only between Americans, but between entire generations of Americans. It is therefore important to understand each program's origin, development, funding strategy, and to have some perspective on the inevitable changes to their future funding. After this primer, we'll return to the implications and impact on minors and their families.

- **Origin and development:** The Social Security Act was established in 1935, with the first monthly payment beginning in 1940. The initial tax rate was 2% of wages, with employers responsible for half of that payment. Since that time, 24 steps of individual rate increases have slowly moved the rate to the current 12.4 % of wages for Social Security and another 2.9% for Medicare for a total of 15.3%, which includes both employee and employer contributions. Most citizens directly see only half of this amount which is what they can see removed directly from wages on their paycheck. There is an equal amount paid by employers, which the employer categorizes within the cost of compensation for employees. It is effectively the same as paying the employee directly and having the government tax all of it from the employee, but it is perceived by the employee as a smaller amount. That clever sleight of hand of splitting the cost between employer and employee was intended to make the cost less perceptible to employees and part of the original design of the system. It was always intended to help to hide the true cost of the tax. That decision was quite clever and effective, since it obfuscates the truth from the citizens who should openly understand what is being taken from them.

In an open democracy it would be proper to be more honest and forthcoming with citizens. Naturally, it is much easier to take $4,600 from a family of 4 making $60,000 per year, than it is to take $9,200 from that same family making $64,600. The employee receives $55,400 in both cases, before the other taxes and deductions are taken out, but that $9,200 might seem very unreasonable to a struggling family, especially when other taxes and benefits costs are considered. The cash flow would be the same for the government, employer and employees, but allowing the citizen to observe the higher amount would better highlight the scale of impact on the family's disposable income and on their lives. Whether this is viewed as a fair or unfair deception depends on whether one believes that citizens can make informed decisions, or instead believes that citizens are not sufficiently capable of making informed decisions, and require government representatives, their advisors and clever experts to make the decisions and package and manage the messaging.

Social Security rates have not changed since 1990, but that doesn't mean that Social Security taxes have not increased.

The maximum earnings taxed has increased greatly, by 148%. Similarly, the tax rate for Medicare has remained the same, but the ceiling to taxable income amount which was once limited to the first $125K of earnings has been eliminated, making all earnings subject to the 2.9% for Medicare.

Social Security has been very successful in reducing poverty among the elderly. In 1935, during the Great Depression, President Franklin Delano Roosevelt's commission reported that over half of the elderly population was poor; later scholarly research indicated that the correct number may have been as high as 78% of elderly in poverty, compared to 68% for the full population of citizens that same year, (Eugene Smolensky, 1987)[18] or 10 percentage points higher than the general population. In stark contrast, today the elderly poverty rate is now 9%, lower than the total population figure of 14%, and much lower than the poverty rate for children of 20%, and below that of ages 19-64 at 12%. In fact, not only has the level of poverty declined below that of the overall population, but the accumulated wealth of seniors has increased substantially relative to all other groups. (Henry J. Kaiser Family Foundation, 2017)[19]

– **Future problems seeded by the initial design**

The concept of Social Security is simple but the implementation details and decision rules of the program are not. At the simplest level, all U.S. employees and employers pay into a pension system through taxes on wages; theoretically, these wages and employer matching payments are invested into a trust fund. When the employee reaches retirement age or retires early, there is a pension fund available from these contributions to pay benefits to the retired worker and spouse. The pension benefits are determined using a formula which uses information on the amount and timing of past contributions, scaling benefits for a higher return per invested dollar to those who contributed less; conversely there is a lower return to those who contributed more, theoretically to allow for the redistribution of benefits to those in higher need.

This concept of funding an investment and receiving returns is simple enough, so what is the problem? The first is embedded in the investment mechanism of the Trust Fund. The program began with the goal of creating a pension for older Americans. However, there was no initial accumulated Trust balance to pay for the benefits of early recipients. There were, however, sufficient funds contributed yearly to support the initial benefits, so the early beneficiaries were not drawing from their investment in the fund but instead were drawing directly from the investment of other citizens. The tax on employees and employer was partly being invested in the Trust Fund but was also diverted and redistributed to the recipients who had also invested, but who invested far less than they were receiving in benefits.

The scale of benefits paid above what was contributed by early participants was a significant redistribution of wealth through the Social Security program. An analysis in the Urban Institutes 2015 report on Social Security and Medicare brings this to a human level by modeling the differences in contribution and funding over the time that Social Security was rapidly growing in funding, benefits, and rates. These models show how the present value of the lifetime contribution and benefits for a married couple who retire at age 65 varies depending on when they turned 65 in the program: Retiring in 1960 ($19K in taxes vs. $222K in benefits): retiring in 1980 ($92 K in taxes vs. $398 K in benefits); 2000 ($203K in taxes vs. $424K in benefits); expected 2020 ($287K in taxes vs. $511K in benefits). (Quakenbush, 2015)[20] Each of these represents large intergenerational redistribution of funds, though never referred to in that way. The system was in fact shifting funds between cohorts or generations of Americans, from younger to older. Of course, nearly none of the tax was directly on minors, but much of it was from the parents of minors whose funds were redistributed, with significant indirect impact on the minors. (The other shift in returns, is less relevant to the vote, which is from those with high earnings to those with lower earnings. This is more widely understood and accepted as part of the design. The higher wage contributors receive a lower return rate on their contribution, comparable to the structure of the graduated U.S. income tax system.)

Funding Scheme – Pyramid, not Ponzi

Social Security funding has long been known to be insufficient to pay planned and promised benefits in the future. In 2018, the combined Social Security Trust funds and the Medicare hospital insurance Trust fund will both be eating into their reserves. Both funds are expected to continue eating into their reserves until reserves are fully depleted, which for Medicare's Hospital Insurance is 2026 and Social Security in 2035. At that time, Social Security would be able to support 91% of costs, using incoming payments, but that would be using funds that should be building the Trust Fund for the employees contributing at that time. Obviously, there will need to be changes to the funding model, which again points to the importance of representation for minors when those decisions are made.

The reason the Trust Fund is insufficient to support employees is because the design shares similarities with a system for building wealth called a pyramid scheme. It is not quite fair to state that it actually is a pyramid scheme, though it certainly does share many characteristics which appeared to be a feature of the design, not a flaw, to the early proponents of the program, since it effectively hides its true mechanisms. These later became more clearly visible as flaws and have a real risk of becoming fatal flaws in the future.

A brief aside on why this design is a problem. Pyramid Scheme refers to a process for building both the infrastructure and cash flow of an entity or organization by constant growth, either in the pool of participants, or the volume of services or products, or both. The pyramid shape is an essential part of the system, because survival depends on growth and the constant entry of new participants funding the returns to the earlier participants. As long as there is growth, there is always enough new money to fuel the future. In recent practice, it typically has involved growing the number of resources actively selling the product or service, while concurrently continuing to sell the product or service. Those early in the process get a portion of the returns from the employees who come in later. So the first employee sells products or services, developing two or more other employees, and those new employees continue to repeat the same process, growing a pyramid below them. As long as each new participant is able to buy inventory and attract other employees, it is a growing business and everyone does well. The higher people in the pyramid do best, on down the line, less so, like any other hierarchy.

For a more detailed example, imagine that person one (P1) has a special soap, they sign up 5 soap distributors who must pay a fee, say a $1,000 training fee and buy $1,000 of soap for inventory to sell and must further develop their own region and establish more distributors. P2-P6, do the same, so we now have 25 new people with soap, and the original 5, so $30K in fees and $30K of soap purchased, with P1 getting a commission on all of the money, and P2-P6 each getting commission on 5 each. Eventually, there is a national network of distributors and lots of inventory. Sometimes this can work, and there are successful corporations that have grown this way and continue to thrive. But often it is the last people in the line who end up with a lot of inventory of soap. The person at the top of the pyramid does very well, but when the pyramid stops growing or collapses there is not sufficient demand for soap to find new customers. The same concept was used in a slightly different way by penny stock boiler rooms, which pump up the price of a stock by buying a lightly traded stock, use the rising price as evidence of underlying value to convince others to buy it...... which is when they begin to unload the stock, and then finally when their shares are sold and no longer supports the price, it drops to its proper value. Those middle participants are left holding a portfolio of low value stock.

It is provocative to underscore the tight similarity between a Pyramid Scheme and the methods used in developing Social Security, but this is not the first time it's been done because the similarity is real. It is provocative but it is accurate and seems to challenge a program that is essential. But understanding this is important to understand the true impact of the program on future generations. The term "scheme" is used here, and will bring to mind a Ponzi Scheme,[21] where there is generally no underlying asset and these should not be confused. A Pyramid Scheme relies on growth but doesn't necessarily rely on a fundamentally fraudulent structure. In the case of Social Security, there is a Trust Fund which does contribute to paying Social Security. However, on the other hand, the fund does not represent the full amount necessary to fund the liabilities that are committed to those who invest in the funds, nor are they separated sufficiently from other funds to guarantee paying an amount to the recipients that is relatively equivalent to a share of the contribution. Public financial services companies are prevented from this kind of behavior and would quickly be charged with financial fraud for using this structure and advertising these promises.

There are differences between Pyramid and Ponzi schemes and the Social Security Systems Structure, but there are also stark similarities: 1) In all of these, the early participants withdrew far more than they ever paid into the system, demonstrating the successful nature of the system and building confidence with everyone; 2) All rely on a proportionally much smaller portion of the population receiving benefits or funds at the top of the pyramid, and therefore depend on a growing pyramid. 3) All use terms consistent with these schemes, for example referring to a trust fund as though it is sitting in cash or securities to create a sense of security for the contributor. There is some truth to the 'trust' since it is holding government securities, but it is also theoretical, since it is writing an IOU to itself. A corporation that wrote a similar note to itself that it kept on a computer with claims to owe itself a trillion dollars would not be permitted to claim to have a trust fund.

A real-world example of the problem is exemplified by the first recipient which is both a success story for the program and an indicator of the potential danger that a price will be paid in the future. The recipient of the first Social Security check number 00-000-001 was Ida May Fuller, in 1940 after paying $25.75 into the system. Ida May continued to receive payments for 35 years until 1975 when she passed away at the age of 100, receiving a total of $22,888.92 in benefits. Ida's generation and generations which followed generally received much more than they paid in – in the same way that a chain letter or any such scheme provides the early participants benefits at the expense of those who follow. Those early generations took the U.S. through the depression and World War II, so it should not be assumed that the initial decision to fund was wrong, it simply shows that as the program has grown, there will someday be a price to pay.

Impact of the change in the nation's age distribution

Beyond the drain of beneficiaries drawing benefits far beyond their contribution which was planned, the improvements in survival rates for older Americans has magnified the size of the problem. As long as the population of the early recipients was small relative to the contributor group, the effect on the Trust fund of beneficiaries receiving benefits beyond their contribution could remain small. That was planned, but what actually happened was more costly. Until very recently and throughout human history with few exceptions, the age distribution of the population was the shape of a triangle or pyramid, with a much larger base of younger people, coming to a smaller point of older people. The two combined forces which create that shape are births, i.e. fertility above replacement, and deaths from disease, war and old age. That triangle or pyramid shape comes to a small triangle at the top of those over 65, coming to a tip for those over 75. Below that is the rest of the large triangle of the population who, in the funding scenario, contribute their wages to support the benefits and build the Trust Fund.

As long as the tip is small relative to the base, funding benefits above contributions for that subgroup of citizens is a manageable problem. However, the emerging challenge to the system is the portion of the pyramid that can no longer be characterized as the 'tip'. The proportional shift is fairly well known and has been changing for some time. In 1940, the portion of the population at that tip, those over 65, was 7 percent; this is now 15 percent and poised to climb to 20 percent in the next 10 years and expected to level at around 22 percent. It may be easier to understand the level of that shift as a ratio of number of recipients compared to the overall population. Those same numbers represent moving from 1 in 14 of the population over 65, to more than 1 in 5. That is 1 in 5 of the population, not 1 in 5 of employed taxpayers. In the early years, the portion of Social Security recipients was an even smaller portion of the tip than the age over 65 indicates. By 1950 only 2% or 1 in 50 of the total population received a social security check, growing to 8% by 1960, 16% by 1980 and nearly 19% by 2015. The Baby Boom generation, those born 1946-1964, will cause these ratios to continue to rise.

> ➤ *Unintended Consequences*

As the scale of Social Security has grown to create larger financial flows, by growth in the number of people covered and in the percent of wages taxed, the program has had some unintended consequences that were not foreseen during at its inception.

 — **Regressive Transfer of Wealth** The Social Security Tax has unintentionally transferred a huge amount of wealth from younger to older Americans, and continues to actively do so to this day. In the 25 years since Social Security and Medicare tax increased to 15%, from 1989 to 2013, the median net worth (in constant 2013 dollars, adjusting for inflation) of the 65+

group experienced an increase of 57% from a median of $136K to $214K per head of household, while the groups aged 45-64 declined 24% from $177K to $136K. Changes in the averages tell a similar story as changes in medians, with the 65+ group improving 72%, and the 45 to 64 group improving 24%. For those 35-44, the group in the highest concentration of young family stage, the same period brought a 51% drop in wealth from a median of $102K to $47K, with the sub-35 adults dropping 30% from a modest $15K to an even more modest $10K. Simply stated, older Americans are getting much wealthier, while at the same time, those at the stage of raising a family struggle to establish basic savings while simultaneously being taxed higher than that older group was at the same stage in their lives.

– **Demographic Group Variance in Lifetime Benefits** - Consistent with the original objectives of the program, Social Security theoretically provides a higher rate of return in benefits to lower income members, and also covers survivor and disability insurance. However, the differences in longevity between demographic groups creates a de facto difference in the lifetime benefits reimbursed to each demographic group. For example, life expectancies at age 65 vary from 20.4 years for white women, and 19.4 years for black women, to 17.8 years for white men and 16.2 years for black men. That means that for two individuals at identical levels of contribution, a white woman would receive 26% higher lifetime return than a black man, and a black woman would receive 9% higher lifetime return than a white man. Each demographic group will have a different profile and therefore different lifetime results for the same investment. Furthermore, since life expectancy is correlated with wealth, this may be another regressive wealth transfer. In the same way, any family or subgroup advantaged by higher longevity will be advantaged by this structure, and similarly any subgroup that suffers from lower longevity will be disadvantaged. There is no obvious solution to this, but it is among the many issues which occur when redistributing wealth within a mandated contribution program.

– **Supplanting support for elderly parent** Beyond direct financial flows, Social Security has had an unintended impact on American families and U.S. culture. Through much of human history, the elderly who were in need might turn to their extended family or their children for assistance. In a sense Social Security was intended to replace the need for that. However, when Social Security began to draw such a high amount of money from the young, it absorbed the discretionary funds which might have been available to assist elderly parents who were in need. The funds were taken and redistributed, not only to the parents who had invested their lives into their children's development and pursuit of happiness, but also to others of the same age, including the rich miser down the road (who might have hoarded his own money, with views of children as 'the surplus population'.) That redistribution is a value destroying change as it replaces a loving exchange with a cold financial transaction. Since it is a fallacy that this is truly a trust fund system, where one invests and is given a return on investment, but is more realistically a pay as you go system, the factor of how many children raised should be included somewhere in the benefits calculation, with at least some additional stipend within Social Security for parents who have raised children paying into the system. This becomes much more important now with childfree selection becoming more common.

To make it more tangible, take a simple example: two people at age 65, both with a $30K salary for a lifetime, the first raised 10 children who now each earn a $40K salary, collectively as a group now paying $60K annually into the system. The second person with the identical salary and work history did not raise children, and therefore was able to save and accumulate more wealth. Both of the people age 65 paid the same into the system, but the one with the children, with less wealth due to investment in the children, is the person who created the wealth which is now funding the current benefits and essentially funding the system, along with the rest of the nation's taxes. This money which would have supplemented the parent's savings is being diverted. In its current form, the system creates an inequitable redistribution away from larger families to individuals or to smaller families. The system does not attempt to recognize the full contribution to the system beyond direct wage. Keep in mind that historically, before the system intervened, the elderly could rely on their family, not the state, for care and support. The state, that is the federal government, is now absorbing those funds and subordinating the decisions that a family might make to the state's decision and ignoring the secondary effects of the changes.

➤ **Social Security Funding Gap** There is a known gap to the future funding of Social Security which must eventually be addressed. The longer the issue is delayed, the more severe the remedy. When Congress finally chooses to openly address this, there is a very high risk that the costs and changes will again increase the heavy demands on young families. It should surprise no citizen that the representatives will do what they were elected to do, which is to represent their constituency. Based on the current distribution of citizens who have the vote, without the proxy, the burden on future generations will increase to the point that the society risks selling the future to make the present easier to manage and govern.

– **Tax rate increases or benefit payment reductions in the future** – The proxy vote will not create any immediate primary change to the Social Security program. American citizens will judge as unfair the proposition of removing the benefits already promised to the older citizens who depend on them. However, the proxy vote may prevent changes to the program that will further jeopardize the protections to their family members and may help resolve the outstanding issues related to insufficient funding. In a 2016 analysis of the future financial budget for Social Security, the Congressional Budget Office (CBO), the nonpartisan federal agency within the legislative branch which provides analysis to Congress, indicated that the Disability Insurance trust fund will be exhausted by 2026 and the remaining OASDI trust fund by 2034. Without change in the current rates, Social Security payments would need to drop across the board by 29%. It is important to consider that this would mean that the Trust Fund would be depleted as well, so everyone approaching retirement would not have the surety of the fund. They would be contributing to Social Security and relying on the next generation to remain committed to it, while worrying that they may decide that they are unwilling to continue to pay into an insecure program. The 29% is already not an acceptable outcome, so the debate will need to begin soon. The establishment of the proxy for minors will force the discussion to happen sooner, since it is future generations that will carry the burden of additional cost. It is important that the young families who will pay into that system but not receive any return for many years, have a fair share of input.

– **Politics of Resolving Social Security Funding Gap** - Social Security is a politically very sensitive topic, perhaps the most politically toxic. It is the most important government program to so many citizens and combined with Medicare spends over 3 times the amount of the next largest spending area of the U.S. government. Yet it is rarely highlighted as an issue by politicians and the media in any election cycle. How is it possible that a program that costs more than any other is rarely discussed? For representatives, any discussion of change or open acknowledgement of future problems is too dangerous a topic. Avoidance is easier.

The impact on the young is extremely high, so it's necessary to discuss this openly soon and some group will need to accept the political fallout. To understand Social Security funding, it is important to expose the clever terminology – especially the 'trust fund', somewhat reminiscent of Newspeak from Orwell's dystopian novel *1984*. It is meant to bring to mind the safety of an increasing financial balance of funds. However, what is actually occurring is the government has already used those funds for discretionary operating expenses. The trust fund is a number on paper which indicates what the government owes itself in Treasury bonds. Since Social Security has been receiving more revenue than it is required to pay to recipients when the demographics were favorable, the money was invested in federal bonds which were sold to itself by the federal government. The fact that this occurs compounds the problem when it shifts to a position where it is no longer in surplus: 1) The government must now raise funds which previously came from the Social Security surplus to meet its normal operating spending and deficits; and 2) the government must find new buyers for more bonds as the Social Security system spending ramps beyond receipts and theoretically redeems its other bonds to make payments.

The Congressional Budget Office highlights the recent crossover point - "In 2010, for the first time since the enactment of the Social Security Amendments of 1983, annual outlays for the program exceeded annual revenues (excluding interest) credited to the combined OASDI trust funds. A gap between those amounts has persisted since then, and in fiscal year 2016, total outlays exceeded noninterest income by about 7 percent."

(Congressional Budget Office , 2017)[22] The Congressional Budget Office 2017 Long Term Budget Outlook indicates that of the $2.9 Trillion in additional debt that will accrue this year, $1.9 Trillion is from Social Security and Medicare, both of which were planned to be self-funding. These will only increase in future years, so we can anticipate that there will soon be proposals to increase these taxes. These taxes will place an additional burden on young families, who already struggle with a difficult economic environment. Without the proxy, they will remain underrepresented in this decision.

– **Economic Impact on the Families of Minors** To understand the impact of Social Security on young families here is a simple thought experiment. Let's outline a micro world and consider the impact of different choices in that world: begin with two example young families and broaden to include the financial impact on a community, and then consider how the proxy vote can create some balance. First the two young-family households – one couple with 3 children and a single parent with 3 children. In each household the adults are 35 years old and household income for each is $45,000, each with a net worth of $40,000, most of that in home equity, all close to the U.S. averages. Each household is paying close to $7,000 (including the 50% company match or self-employment tax) annually into Social Security and Medicare. They are paying into a future retirement fund for the next 30 years from now. They are paying into this on the promise that the money is being invested and will be there in 30 years, but we already know that the trust fund will be depleted in that 30 years. Whether the generations that come later will grow sufficiently and financially sound enough to cover their payments is a hope that cannot be guaranteed.

The first question: If the decision to pay into the Social Security system was optional, would it be a good decision for these families to pay into that system? Stated differently, is the decision a good investment choice at this time for their family's development? Another spin on the same question: If asked for advice on their decision, would you advise them to invest in a retirement plan that is not guaranteed and to invest so much of discretionary funds at age 35, when they have a young family with immediate needs? Should the nation compel this choice for someone in this situation? Perhaps it might be a better choice to invest for retirement in their 40's? Or it might it be more sensible to only invest when there is an ironclad guarantee, where the funds are up to date with no possibility of getting behind the curve in the Trust fund's ability to pay benefits.

Some form of tax increase will inevitably be approved rather than reduce benefits and it is a waiting game until there is enough concern raised by citizens to require representatives to bring the issue to the floor (without being punished for taking a position on the issue). It may be that the issue will await a time of a boom economy when the pain of the increase is lower. The proxy vote would not likely change the outcome, which will be a requirement for additional taxes, but it may create a more balanced approach to deciding who pays for the increase. Congress might begin to consider more creative alternatives than a straight wage-based increase that has such a high impact on families and has the effect of being a regressive tax system.

————

Beginning with a blank slate when considering these realities: is it fair to tax these young families who need the money for launching their lives to redistribute it to the older families who have higher accumulated wealth? With a proxy vote, it is not clear that dramatic changes would be made to offset the forced choice, but it is certain that government representatives would be more careful about how the added costs are distributed, with more protection of the young family.

3) Medicare and Medicaid – Medicare spending of $700 Billion and Medicaid of nearly $600 Billion, equate to roughly $4350 in annual spending per citizen, or $17,400 per family of 4. As with Social Security, there is a long history of Medicare changes which is not well known or understood by most citizens. Medicare is commonly believed to be paid for by working citizens along with the federal payroll tax deductions known as FICA (Federal Insurance Contributions Act) and OASDI (Old age, survivor and disability insurance) with the Medicare portion as stated in the deduction of 1.45% and matched by the employer with 1.45%. As with Social Security, most believe there is a deposit into an appreciating asset, so that when they become seniors, they will simply be receiving the returns back on what they have paid into the system. These beliefs are even less correct for Medicare than they are for Social Security.

Medicare is the single payer national health insurance system which serves Americans over 65 and disabled Americans. The program was enacted by Congress in 1965 in Title XVIII of the Social Security Act to offer health insurance to people age 65 and older, regardless of income or medical history. The coverage has expanded several times since then, adding benefits for speech, physical, and chiropractic therapy in the 1970s, payments to HMO's in the 1980s now under Medicare Part C, expanding to include eligibility for younger people with permanent disabilities, those who receive Social Security Disability Insurance payments, and those who have end-stage renal disease. It expanded again in the early 2000's covering all drugs under Medicare Part D. The original payment into OASDI began as 0.7% split with employer and employee and has increased over the 54 years in 8 steps to 2.9%. In addition, beginning in 2013, an additional 0.9% is taxed on incomes above $200K for single taxpayers and above $250K for married households. It is not indexed, therefore it will continue to grow as it captures an increasing portion of the income of middle class Americans as inflation drives wages higher over time.

The Part A portion of Medicare providing hospital inpatient and nursing coverage, is paid for by the same year's contributions through the payroll tax. In a sense, that leaves an unfunded liability since most working contributors believe that they are paying into a fund. The results up to now have been that each recipient is receiving far more than they've paid in. For example, for a couple turning 65 in 2015, making an average wage of $47,800, Medicare lifetime contributions would be $70,000, compared to total $422,000 in lifetime benefits, an excellent financial result for them. Similarly, the group that turned 65 in 2000, paid in $39,000 and received $308,000 in benefits. The 2025 group, those born in 1960, will have paid in $84,000 and receive $547,000 in lifetime benefits. So, everyone is receiving more than they paid in. In real life, money doesn't magically appear, so it must be coming from somewhere and that somewhere is that it is being borrowed from someone else's future benefits or from the tax payment that would have previously funded all other federal programs. (Quakenbush, 2015)[23]

Although the Part A portion of Medicare is covered by payroll deductions from that year, Part B and D which combine for $393.4 Billion in 2016, are only partially paid for by premiums with the remaining amounts covered by the Federal Government general budget, which required $319.2 Billion from the general budget in 2016. (The Board of Trustess of the Federal Hospital Insurance and Federal Supplementay Insurance Trust Fund, 2017)[24]

Medicare has been highly successful in making affordable medical coverage available to seniors. The program is well regarded by seniors, with 80% of the 65+ group indicating that Medicare is working well for most seniors according to a 2013 survey. (Foundation, 2013)[25] Discussion of change or criticism of Medicare is politically dangerous to representatives due to the threat of offending their 65+ constituency. The Heritage Foundations report, Medicare's Next 50 Years: Preserving the Program for Future Retirees, reviews the full set of issues, some of which are sometimes covered in the public press: gaps in coverage; waste, fraud, and abuse; interference with physician's professional independence; restriction of patient freedom; and extreme and overwhelming bureaucracy imposed on doctors and hospitals. The issues which might be affected by the proxy vote are related to the rising costs and the impact of future increases in government spending and implications for the government debt, so we'll touch upon these here.

> ➤ **Future Rate Increases** - The 2017 Annual Report of Medicare's Trust Fund Boards of Trustees (Federal Hospital Insurance and Supplementary Medical Insurance) indicates that the Medicare Part A (the hospital insurance portion paid through deductions) would have sufficient revenue to pay expenses until 2028 and will then fall short. To support the longer-term forecast, an increase from the current rate of 2.9%, to a new higher rate of 3.64% would permit the program to remain solvent through the 75-year forecast period. The realistic scenario is that the increase will not be immediate, and therefore will require a steeper level of increase. (The Board of Trustess of the Federal Hospital Insurance and Federal Supplementay Insurance Trust Fund, 2017)[26]
>
>   Medicare Part B and D present a different and somewhat larger problem. Since any expenses above the premiums are paid for through the federal budget, they will theoretically never fall short of funds over the longer term. However, that spending increase must be made up through the federal budget, either through increasing taxes, by continuing to increase the Federal Deficit, or by reducing funding of other government agencies. In 2016 these programs combined for $393.4 Billion in paid benefits, against $86 Billion or 22% paid for by premiums, with the remainder covered through the Federal Budget. By comparison, the 2016 general revenue portion of Medicare was equivalent to 15.7% of all personal and corporate income taxes, therefore increasing the Federal Debt; it is planned to continue to grow to 21.1% by 2030. Another comparison is that this single line item portion of Medicare, which comes from the Federal Budget and covers a portion of the population, is around half

what the United States pays for the defense of the nation each year. The natural effect of its continued growth will be to crowd out other discretionary programs, like education, defense, etc., and continue to build the Federal Debt and the corresponding interest payments on the Federal Debt.

➤ **Closer look at the Impact on the Young** Medicare is highly successful from the perspective of seniors who express a high rate of satisfaction with a large and complex program. It began at a time when only 60% of seniors had health insurance, primarily due to cost and availability. It has clearly met the original objective of providing health insurance to those 65 and older, regardless of income or medical history. It has also become a commitment that was not originally intended to generate so much of the nation's health costs and absorb so much of the nation's budget. Planners have consistently underestimated the costs of Medicare, especially in forecasting the increasing cost of medical care. Some of that increased cost came through the innovation in equipment, medicine, and the overall cost of therapy, and some as the result of the success in increasing life expectancy at age 65, moving from the early forecasting days of Medicare, when it was 79.7 to 85.5; This increases the years of coverage from 14.7 years to 20.5 years, a 40% increase in covered years on Medicare.

The issue for the impact on young families is primarily financial, through future higher taxes on the parents of minors and through the diminishing funding of government activities which might have been of benefit to them. The overwhelming majority of the program is directed to senior citizens who receive substantially higher average benefits than they have paid into the program. The result is that the money is borrowed from the both the present, crowding out other potential government choices, and borrowed from the future in building up the Federal Deficit. The level of expense per full time employee, excluding the Part B and D premiums, is equivalent to $4700 per employee, which theoretically could be used by young families. The same issues emerge here as were discussed for Social Security. Since the 65+ group has the highest net worth, is the income redistribution from younger to the older Americans fair? Whether it comes in the form of crowding other items in the federal budget or building up the Federal Debt, the young family will at some point bear most of the additional costs. Repeating a similar set of questions as for Social Security:

Since Medicare is not actually funded by an invested balance, but rather a redistribution from one generation to another, is it fair to force redistribution of the income of the young families with lower net average net worth and a longer term future requirement of supporting themselves and their family, to provide funds for older adults who have higher net worth and fewer other responsibilities?

- Is it fair to build the Federal Debt, which will inevitably be left to the next generation?
- Beginning with a clean slate, would it be fair to tax these young families who need the money for launching their lives to redistribute more of it to the healthcare of older families who have higher wealth?

The proxy vote will not change the current taxation of these families, but it may encourage government representatives to be more careful about how the future increase in costs is distributed, with a possible bias towards more caution about extracting funds from the young family.

4) Unfunded Pension Liabilities – Pension liabilities represent the value of funds which would be invested to support the benefits promised to state and local government employees through promises made during contract negotiation of wages and benefits. The calculation method which determines the level of liability varies by state, and changes over time. The calculated liabilities are based on estimates of many variables into simple mathematical formulas to determine the amount owed into the future. These variables include the number of years to retirement, salary increases, worker longevity, etc. The total pension liability in 2016 was just short of $4 Trillion. (The Pew Charitable Trusts, 2016)[27] That number represents the amount that would be owed now by each U.S. citizen to pay for the pension plans for the work already completed to date by state government employees. It is what each citizen owes for the work of the past, not for the current year. It is also not future liability for future work, but rather, it is the liability for completed work. Most of the money to fund these future payments has been paid into the state pension systems and therefore there are existing pension fund assets already in place to fund much of these liabilities. Using plan administrator calculations, the funded amount is $2.6 Trillion of the $4 Trillion. The assumptions used by some systems lean towards optimistic returns on invested funds compared to history, which would mean that the real gap is larger than it appears. However, even with those assumptions, there remains $1.4 Trillion in "unfunded liability", meaning if all U.S. citizens were liable for this funding, the average family of four would owe $18,400 in unfunded liability to state workers. To repeat, these are for commitments already made and for the work that was already done in the past.

The unfunded liability varies widely by state, making the $18,400 per family of four a less accurate way to view the liability. Most families face no future problem from these liabilities, while others face a huge problem. For example, the worst state, New Jersey, has an unfunded pension liability of $21,200 per citizen or $84,800 for a family of four. This is in a state with a median household income of $73.2K – so each family of four essentially owes more than a year's pretax compensation for pension commitments that were made in the past by state government representatives.[28] (The United States Census Bureau, 2012) New Jersey's funded and unfunded liabilities combine to $30,600 per citizen or $122,400 for a family of four. Running a distant, but still shocking, second in unfunded liabilities is Illinois with $12,100 per citizen or $48,400 for a family of four for commitments already made. Since these are commitments already made but not funded, the money eventually must come from these citizens. Eventually it will mean higher taxes, income taxes that will affect investment, real estate taxes to extract the value from homeowners with a consequent reduction in the value of property, and lower government service levels, reducing school support or support for other essential services. Consistent with these liabilities, New Jersey and Illinois were ranked 48th and 50th in fiscal solvency by the Mercatus Center.[29] (Mercatus Center George Mason University, 2018)

On the other side of the spectrum among states is Wisconsin, which is essentially fully funded, followed closely by South Dakota and Tennessee, each having below $425 per citizen in unfunded liabilities. The relevance to the proxy vote of these unfunded liabilities should be obvious. The liabilities already committed must either be paid or pushed to the following generation. How that is done and what that spending displaces will have significant implications for minors and their families. Perhaps more important, the tendency to negotiate government employee benefits without considering the longer-term impact of these costs on future generations, as done in New Jersey and Illinois, will continue without the balance of representation for that future generation.

5) Health Insurance and the Affordable Care Act – The Affordable Care Act (ACA) was conceived to expand the availability of healthcare to many who were unable to buy insurance due to affordability or availability, primarily due to pre-existing conditions. The program has been an area of conflict, since even before it was enacted in 2010, with political parties, lobbyists, and special interest groups forming moving battle lines on different aspects of the program. The broader conflict over where to draw a line on government involvement in the health care system and whether intervention in the private system is a public good has a longer history, with similar alignment between parties and interest groups. Most informed adult citizens have an opinion on this, and this discussion does not seek to examine the alternatives or evaluate its effectiveness to date. Instead it seeks to highlight the ACA as a stunning and clear example of how the lack of representation for minors resulted in young families as the target to absorb the higher costs in implementing the Act, through both the individual mandate and community rating which were both known to increase the cost of the policies of younger citizens to supplement the cost of the insurance of older Americans.

The first challenge for the ACA, and arguably its brightest achievement, was closing the gap on the lack of availability of insurance to citizens with preexisting conditions and eliminating the risk of lost insurance coverage for those who have higher cost histories. Prior to implementation of the ACA, insurance companies would often deny coverage to those with significant preexisting conditions, because the high cost of providing benefits would require unsustainable pricing to these customers. On the other hand, not eliminating these customers from the general risk pool would require increasing pricing to the entire pool, making the insurance company's pricing uncompetitive compared to insurance companies which did deny coverage for preexisting conditions. One solution which had been in place in several states for small group and small company policies, was "guaranteed-issue", which required insurers to cover everyone in the group, not permitting exclusion of those with pre-existing conditions, by raising overall costs of these pools or causing a loss for the insurance companies.

The ACA prevents insurance companies from using health status or medical history information in determining rates. All health plans must cover treatment for pre-existing conditions from the day coverage begins. Therefore, the higher cost of those who have already been identified as high cost will naturally raise the cost of all insurance. By eliminating the health history and pre-existing conditions screens, the cost of insurance goes up - but a second problem also arises. That problem is that a clever individual could forgo insurance, saving the premium fees until they require more costly medical care or are diagnosed with a medical condition, and then subscribe to an insurance plan, therefore avoiding paying the insurance premiums needed to fund benefits. For many, it would be economically sound to choose to wait until there was a need for treatment. That would drive up rates, since insurance company revenue for these individuals would only come in at times when they know their medical expenses would exceed their insurance payments. This dilemma led to the concept and requirement for an insurance mandate.

The second significant issue solved within the ACA was the high cost of insurance and healthcare for the group of older Americans who are still below the age of eligibility for Medicare. Since young citizens are on average healthier than their older fellow citizens, younger Americans require fewer healthcare services, fewer high cost services, and have fewer chronic conditions which are the primary drivers of higher healthcare costs. Under normal insurance market conditions, cost history indicates that the cost of benefits to insure a typical 64-year-old would be approximately 6 times the cost of an 18-year-old. Before the ACA, a small number of states had attempted to address this by requiring 'community rating', mandating that insurance companies establish equivalent premiums within a given geographic area without regard to their age or medical conditions. Other states attempted a modified form of community rating, creating a limit to the multiple between the highest and lowest cost policy, therefore raising the cost of the young and healthy to lower the cost of the older and less healthy. This was the approach which was repeated in the ACA, which has applied a maximum factor of 3 to 1 as the range of difference allowable in cost between insurance policies. The result is an increase in the cost of policies to the young and a decrease for older Americans.

This may seem a practical approach; someone might conclude that the moderate increases in the cost of insurance to the young to allow a decrease in cost for older (even though often wealthier) Americans is fine. However, the cost increases for the young are more substantial and cannot be considered moderate. There are many articles which describe and simulate the impact of the ACA on younger adults and the elderly, and two of the most direct of those are included in the footnotes.[30] (Carlson, 2013) (Roy)[31] There was no full capture of actual detailed effects on the individual age groups when this document was completed, but a rough calculation indicates a range of approximately 75% increase in cost increase for younger adults.

The combination of the two solutions of 1) eliminating screening for preexisting conditions and 2) raising prices for younger adults beyond the natural cost levels, both directly raised prices for young families to pay for older and wealthier Americans. In both cases, it becomes a good decision for the healthy young citizen to not purchase health care until they have a diagnosed illness or accident. This leads to the requirement for the mandate. The mandate was intended to address this, by imposing a penalty that grows over time, and with income, and with the number of members in the family, and had been in place since 2014. Enrollments for the young continued to lag planned levels resulting in even higher than expected costs for ACA insurance coverage. The individual mandate was eventually repealed within the 2017 Tax Cut and Jobs Act.

The Affordable Care Act is a good example of how lack of the representation for minors can result in the government making decisions which ignore what is in the best interest of minors and the young family. Within the controversy surrounding the implementation, it is shocking to note the ease with which the young adults and young families were used to improve the risk pool for the older Americans, and for those with pre-existing conditions, which also have a higher concentration of older Americans. The act of creating these pools and the mandate is clearly a forced redistribution of wealth to older Americans who tend to be wealthier. The group that also has lower immediate and long term demands on that wealth.

The insurance mandate is a good example of a terrible redistributive policy that is determined by the power in the voting group, making it a requirement for young people to buy insurance which by law is designed to be over-priced to those young citizens. It is a tax for being young and for not having the advocacy of a savvy political interest group comparable to the AARP. The stated objectives of the ACA were to reduce the number of people that did not have health insurance, but the issue of not having health insurance skews heavily to the young. Instead of making it more attractive and affordable, the ACA solved the problem by compelling or requiring them to sign up through the mandate, overriding free choice. The counter argument has been that the government will pay a portion of the premiums for those who cannot afford them, but that goes back to increasing Federal Debt which will eventually rest again upon those same young Americans. Though the government may be supplementing their payment, they are doing so with money that will be owed by that same group of citizens. The ACA and the future process of amendments to the ACA along with the newly emerging government healthcare proposals, represent an excellent example of why the proxy is needed soon!

———

The five areas which were just reviewed – National Debt, Social Security, Medicare, Unfunded Liabilities, and the Affordable Care Act – are each major categories of concern for government representatives. Each has a different and separate process of periodic review of the associated spending, and most provide visibility to citizens through an annual budget review process. These reviews generally provide for limited immediate impact, since many of these are driven by past decisions which determine the starting point and the spending and funding levels. It is a long process to change the status of these. Each begins the year with a balance or set of promised benefits, leaving only small areas of immediate spending that can be affected. The ACA and associated health insurance also receive annual scrutiny through the distributed rate setting process and scrutiny by the press and both political parties, as debate over the future structure of government participation in health insurance remains unsettled. Unfunded liabilities receive less frequent, more ad hoc attention and will continue to do so until there is more citizen insistence that they be addressed.

6) Tax policy – Cutting across all of the areas we just discussed are complex and often opaque government funding processes and tax policies which determine how programs are funded. This sixth area of discussion covers Tax Policy, examining the reasoning for who should pay for the promises.

Taxation is composed of a dog's breakfast of types of taxes, rate schedules, exemptions, and different layers of governmental tax, all seeking to capture a slice of the activities of every citizen, non-citizen, and organization. The list is long: Income for Federal, State and Local, Excise (alcohol, gasoline, cigarettes, soda), Real Estate, Capital Gains, Social Security, Medicare, Alternative Minimum Tax, Sales Tax, County Tax, Transfer Tax, Utilities Tax (phone, electricity, water), Business, Inheritance (Death), Gift, Hotel Tax, Licenses, innumerable Fees, Tariffs (on international trade), Development Assessments, and Tolls. There are so many types of taxes and so much variation in what an individual will pay depending on where and how they live, that it is nearly impossible to know what a citizen has actually paid in taxes for any given year. Most know that there are many taxes and realize that the Federal government depends on the Federal Income tax and Social Security/Medicare for the largest portion of federal funding, 81.4% in 2018. **It is beyond the scope of this book to be in any way comprehensive in discussing this, but it is worthy of a brief examination of taxation from the perspective of a family with minors, to lead to a brief discussion of the impact of the lack of a vote.**

Each area of government tax policy has a large ecosystem of groups involved in influencing its direction and future. The ecosystems include a group of citizens who have a personal stake in the direction of policy and generally are represented by interest groups that represent those citizens on that issue. There are many organizations which also have an interest – including corporations, unions, powerful single-issue interest groups, public sector unions, political parties, political action committees, government agencies, and others - all with a stake in many of the tax policy decisions. Therefore, influence on each decision is driven by this group of diverse interests rather than more directly by constituents.

The process for establishing and modifying taxes varies by government entity, with each round of change following a disparate set of negotiation processes which are usually opaque by necessity, but with many powerful forces pulling in different directions. Since even small changes in rates, exemptions, and government collections can have a large financial impact, tax policies are extensively influenced by powerful interest groups through lobbying and media alignment. For the elected representatives and political parties, as well as for those seeking office, it can be an area of maneuvering and grandstanding, often aligned with a platform viewpoint or longer-term alignment to specific interest groups. It's not surprising that this may be the most contentious battleground of the leading political parties, with continuous skirmishes on many dimensions of taxation: reduction or increase in the level; how the tax increases with income; the type of taxes including the amounts and limitations on exemptions; tax credits; the various interest treatments; the debt limit; sequester; etc. Any sizable change to policy requires political concessions, deal making, negotiation between the political parties and between the members within each party, and with continuous heightened lobbying and scrutiny by the applicable special interest groups and political action committees. The fact that there are so many options and choices for how citizens will be taxed creates greater power for representatives who must then be influenced, since they have the power to decide the winners and losers across the nation. The many groups who want to be among the winners will attempt to influence the representatives, so the only balance for citizens is the power of their vote. Here the lack of representation for minors creates a tremendous gap in fairness, since they are not truly constituents in the sense that they cannot vote, so their power against the special interest groups is exactly zero other than a secondary effect through other constituents.

The combination of the myriad types of taxes, rates, thresholds and exemptions makes it impossible for any citizen to know how much they have paid to the government in taxes each year. The process of establishing taxes is distant from most citizens except those few that happen to be tax experts and those who are employed by the applicable special interests and lobby groups. The best opportunity for citizens to influence tax policy is more indirectly through alignment within the interest groups and through their choice of political party. The full examination of U.S. tax policy is beyond the scope of this discussion, but since these policies have a large impact on young family disposable income, it's worthy of a brief survey of the most relevant areas.

* **Tax policy for Social Security and Medicare Taxes** – Social Security and Medicare decisions were discussed earlier, but let's return to the tax policy side of these programs and how they affect minors and their families. Beginning with the proposition that the government that was created to serve The People, one might consider this question: Is it in the best interest of so many of the people to be compelled to 'save' for retirement, when they are so young and have the immediate needs of the young family? To consider a real example, let's return to the family with a single 35-year old adult raising 3 minors and an income of $40,000 per year. Their forced savings or investment in the Social Security and Medicare system is over $6,000 annually. If there was no existing Social Security and Medicare system, would you advise the adult to take $6,000 of their income and place it in a lockbox that they cannot access for 32 years?

Many citizens might conclude that it is more practical, and prudent to retain these funds for the needs of the family. That additional $6,000 would increase that family's discretionary income by 60%, from approximately $10,000 to $16,000, a huge impact on a young family. The current tax policy does not allow this practical choice as an option, extracting this large amount of discretionary income without regard to the family's situation. It removes an important decision about how and when to save for retirement, transferring the decision from the citizen to the government, and making a burdensome and unreasonable decision for the young family. It is a bad choice, at least one that most reasonable people would not choose without coercion.

While there may be some who would save in this way, most would consider a parent concerned with saving for that distant old age while their children have immediate needs to be something of a miser. (In fact, it is the nation which forces exactly this hidden miserly decision). This approach to extracting funds for old age benefits leaves children with fewer resources to support their development to meet a distant goal. Requiring a 30-year delay of access to funds is something that no successful business would choose, yet we require it of every young parent with very limited resources. It is a bad decision but one that is convenient to meet the requirements of more powerful constituent forces. It is evidence of the lack of the power of the vote that representatives do not seem to notice that this is exactly the set of demands that we have placed upon young families.

This example actually understates the issue because it begins with the premise that the funds are actually being saved for those parents, and relies on the lockbox. But the lockbox is not where that money is going. As stated, and repeated earlier, the lockbox is commonly viewed as a deposit into an asset that is saved or gaining value, and that seniors are simply receiving the returns back on what they have paid into the system. Since that view is not correct, it is possible that future generations either cannot - or decide they will not - support the funding at the same levels. Remember that until now, the recipients of Social Security have been receiving more in net present value than they paid in, meaning they received money by borrowing from future generations. For example, the average married couple turning 65 in 1960, paid in $19K in taxes and received $222K in lifetime benefits. The group turning 65 in 2000, paid in $203K and received $424K. The 2025 group, those born in 1960, will have paid in $308K and receive $542K. It should surprise no one that since everyone is receiving more than they paid in, the money must be borrowed from somewhere; that somewhere is someone else's future.

There are many potential ways to resolve this gap. For example, rather than considering raising the minimum wage, would it not be simpler to exempt a certain amount of everyone's earnings from Social Security and Medicare taxes to allow for a full living wage, scaled for family size, before taxing funds? Does it make sense to remove funds from someone's paycheck, then require that they receive government assistance through food stamps, section 8 housing or other programs? By exempting the first $20-30K of earnings from Social Security and Medicare, an immediate increase of 15% would flow to everyone with no risk of reducing employment due to changing employer economics, in the way that most economists agree that raising the minimum wage would. Of course, the shortfall in Social Security and Medicare would need to be made up elsewhere, probably through higher rates or higher income limits for others, or an increase in the age that new beneficiaries begin to receive benefits.

Another solution would be for the government to extend the time before older Americans begin to seek benefits by increasing employment options for older Americans, therefore reducing the dependence on Social Security. As longevity increases and the quality of older Americans health improves, this becomes increasingly important. This has been a highly neglected opportunity to date, even though the laws are in place to begin to solve this problem. The nation has long tolerated age discrimination in hiring, in a way that it does not permit discrimination based on race or gender. The Age Discrimination in Employment Act (ADEA) has been in place for over 50 years clearly prohibiting age discrimination, yet age discrimination is commonly and openly practiced in most organizations. In a 2017 survey of those age 45 and older, fully 61% stated that they had seen or experienced age discrimination in the workplace. Of those, 90 percent stated it is common or somewhat common.[32] (Commission, 2018) If we are to reduce the long-term costs of Social Security, the United States Equal Employment Opportunity Commission (EEOC) must be empowered, funded, and compelled to actively pursue age discrimination until companies adapt to a new standard. This is a well-known issue that has been nearly ignored by the media and government, though it is unclear why this is the case. In fact, it is so common that a 2018 report by the EEOC [35], concluded that "today, age discrimination is more like, than different from, other forms of discrimination."

The tests that Federal courts have erected to prove that age was the barrier to employment are much different than the standard used to prove sex, race, or religious discrimination, making it difficult to prove and therefore discouraging any legal challenges to employers. It is up to Congress to change the rules to fix this to enable more aggressive enforcement, and up to the Executive branch through the EEOC to enforce them. As life expectancy continues to increase, the nation must not allow older Americans to be discriminated against when seeking employment. This should not be a controversial recommendation, but there is no catalyst to bring this group of Americans together and no special interest group with a priority to lead the charge. It requires a political party to recognize and champion this issue.[33] (Farrell, 2018)

* **Tax policy for Higher Education** – Another category where tax policy fails to balance the needs of minor citizens and their families are the many tax and government policies designed to support Higher Education. Many aspects of higher education tax policy serve more to satisfy the interests of higher education institutions and other special interests, rather than to serve the needs for greater knowledge and education of citizen-students or to provide for broader benefits to the general population of citizens. The policy issues are complex and interrelated, but to make it somewhat easier to examine, the issues will be discussed separately here. This is not intended to be a complete discussion since the issues are complex and interrelated, but this example set of policy failures are enough to make the point that lack of representation creates a neglect of the interests of this group of citizens.

* **Deductibility of tuition and living expenses** – Fair treatment of education expenses would allow related expenses to be deductible on par with the way that businesses are able to deduct their investments in capital. Businesses are able to depreciate an asset over time and are also able to carry net operating losses forward in time to reduce their tax liability. Approaching the investment in education in this way would require that tax policy be changed to allow a student's investment in education to be written off against their future earnings in the future. The student-citizen must invest a large amount of money for tuition and living expense, along with foregoing income for several years, however, under current tax policy, the student does not receive the same favorable tax benefits that a corporation would receive on an investment by writing the investment off over time against future earnings and accumulated financial losses. This

is inconsistent and unfair and gives companies a benefit that it does not allow for citizens.

Similarly, the fact that the student has lost years of income during their education could be better handled by allowing income averaging or another mechanism for their early years of work, to adjust for the progressive income tax rates which force them into higher rates before they have a chance to catch up to what they have invested. For example, the person who forgoes college and makes $300,000 by making $30,000 per year of taxable income over 10 years, will pay a much lower tax than someone who during the same ten years makes $300,000, but does so by investing $150,000 and 6 years into education, and making $75,000 per year for 4 years. They have the same income over the 10 years, but the graduate has a much higher tax liability, on top of a boatload of debt. Tax policy should not be designed to treat one as better than the other.

* **Fairness to all young adult citizens including those that do not attend college**

Not every citizen needs or wants to pursue college or any form of higher education. In the US, the high school graduation rate is 84%, with 66% of those graduating high school eventually going to college. Sixty percent of those entering public 4-year colleges graduate within 5 years. The combination of those statistics yields 33% of the cohort completing a bachelor's degree, consistent with census bureau data for Americans 25 and older. There are *some* good reasons for the government to support the pursuit of further education for all students, but since higher education loan programs act as a transfer of funds from the government to individual citizens, it is only fair to create some balance for the citizens who choose not to pursue higher education, therefore reducing the biased incentive to pursue education when it is not necessarily the best direction for that citizen. If the government is to supplement the funds for the college bound, what justification is there to not provide the equivalent to those not bound for college?

To get specific, if government loan programs provide room and board funding for 4 years for pursuit of a college degree, why shouldn't the same loan program be equally available to the trade school student or the young entrepreneur or any employed worker? If the government is to fund room and board for extended education, there is no reason to withhold this same level of funding to others launching their lives. There may be reasons that one believes it safer to fund education – possibly that students are less likely to default, but the current funding mechanism does not consider the risk of default as a factor in deciding who receives the loans. The lower quality bachelor's degrees, which are known to provide lower economic value, are funded no differently by the government, and that funding results in high levels of debt for those graduates, so why is it better to do that than to provide a plumber's apprentice with a stipend?

Under the current financial aid regime, the government transfers value through subsidized student loans to young people, encouraging them to pursue degrees, which don't always improve their future prospects. Remembering that fully 40% of those entering do not graduate, there are many young adults encouraged to build debt that will be a burden to them. The schools receive the benefit and the student and government foots the bill. Better to simply give every young American a $20-40 thousand stipend when turning age 18, which they can use for room and board, to start a business or waste as some will. If repayment is needed to balance the budget, future earnings could be taxed back to correspond to the amount that was loaned.

The point is not to suggest that the government should or should not provide this stipend, which is a different consideration, but if it chooses to provide the money for one large subset of young citizens, it should do so for the rest of their cohort. It should not be in the business of supplementing the Higher Education industry and the academically more gifted, at the cost of young adults who choose a different path.

* **Student Loan Interest** – student loan interest deductions also phase out as compensation increases. Since a correct view of the interest is as part of an investment and as a normal business deduction, there is no reason to phase out student loan interest deductions.

* **Deductions for college tuition** – the deduction for college tuition is limited to $4K and phases out for parents with higher income levels. As mentioned earlier, the student (or possibly parents who pay the tuition) should receive a tax deduction, in the same way that a business would receive a deduction for an investment, either capitalized or as a period expense. Ideally that tax deduction would be given to the student for use against future income. Providing the tax breaks directly against the student's future earnings, instead of to parents, prevents the application of this tax deduction or tax shield by wealthy and indulgent parents who are willing to finance a 4-year walkabout for their children. It is easy enough for the 4 years to be a long party, not a serious pursuit of education, but with the appearance, prestige and tax benefits of higher education. Witness the 2019 college admission scandal and the donor list of many universities.

Alternatively, one could maintain some tax deduction for parents, but continue to limit the income level at which it applies to avoid the same issue of the tax shield to the indulgent parent. The reason to provide relief for parents is simply to acknowledge that they have provided a financial 'service to the state' by preparing the child for college. It can be argued that preparation and the payment of tuition offers a substantial benefit to the nation, so a fair system would account for that. On average, higher education increases the average lifetime earnings for graduates and those earnings will be taxed by the government, funding Social Security and Medicare, and the full complement of other federal and state expenses. The graduate is also less likely to require financial assistance from other government programs. By paying for the student's college, parents are reducing the longer-term financial burden of student loans on the student, making it more possible that the student can afford to have children or get married or both, again supporting the nation's future.

This discussion is not to propose a decision on any one of these ideas, but rather to highlight that there are many alternatives which would be better for families with minors, and each citizen should have a vote to choose representatives to pursue tax policies that support their interest.

- **Other Tax Policies** – Most of the remaining tax policies are developed with far less consideration for the impact on families with children than their proportion of society would provide under full representation of citizens. Debate over changes to tax policy tends to focus on a few issues, like differentiating the relative effect between differing income levels, its effect on the financial markets, followed by the impact on the Federal Debt. The focus on the young family remains well behind these, though both political parties claim it as a top priority. Here are some of the areas where there is significant lack of consideration of the impact on citizens under age 18, and therefore effecting the family:
  o **Excise and other consumption taxes** – (fuel, tobacco, aviation, alcohol, soda, utilities, etc.) - Excise and consumption taxes are economically attractive because instead of taxing the results of productivity (or income) or of savings (capital gains or interest), they tax consumption, so they avoid

discouraging activities that are good for the economy, like working and investing capital. However, consumption taxes are regressive, meaning that lower income citizens spend a higher percentage of their income on consumption taxes than higher income citizens, and therefore young families pay higher on average. These taxes are often less visible since they are often embedded in the cost of products.

For example, fuel tax of $37.4 Billion annually, or roughly $125 annually per U.S. citizen is embedded in the cost of gasoline and diesel. Every product transported with trucks has a small amount of that fuel tax in its cost. The more visible fuel tax is in the cost of automobile gasoline. The ACA excise tax of $16.3 Billion or $54 per U.S. citizen was paid by the insurance companies to reduce ACA costs, with that cost passed back as embedded in everyone's insurance, with another 2.32% of medical device cost and another $3B upon foreign prescription drug manufacturers and importers. Tobacco and alcohol, the two major "sin taxes" combined for $24B in federal tax and apply directly to the products that are viewed as having a negative impact on society. Aviation taxes of $14B applies directly to those who chose to fly, with 90% relating to passenger and the remainder to transport of goods. Although some of these are regressive taxes to young families, there is no easily apparent solution to reducing these. Fuel taxes properly discourage excessive use of gasoline, as do the alcohol and tobacco taxes, and seem practical to help offset broader societal costs.

o **Sales Taxes** – Sales taxes are also regressive and therefore tax young families disproportionally to the general population. Only 5 states do not have a state sales tax, with the rest ranging from 4% to California's 7.25%. When local taxes are included sales tax can reach above 10%. State and local sales taxes across the nation combined for 35% of state and local funding across the U.S. in 2007, with another 30% from property tax, 27% from individual and corporate income tax, and with the remaining 8% from licenses and fees. Since sales tax is known to be a regressive tax, several states exempt selected goods such as food and other items considered necessities, with several constitutions imposing limitations on these taxes. For the young family, this would be the right improvement across all states, i.e., including tax exemption for food (not prepared food, so excluding restaurants), clothing below a certain price per item, prescription and non-prescription drugs, and possibly select education related items.

o **Real Estate Taxes** – Real estate property taxes, can also be regressive and more directed to families since families require more physical space and have the need to live in areas with better schools which tend to correlate with higher prices for the real estate. Families who rent pay indirectly for those real estate taxes since the landlord who must pay those taxes must transfer the cost into the price of rent. An idea that is similar to real estate tax is the recently proposed tax on net wealth. The concept is that instead of taxing one particular asset, real estate, the tax is spread across the full asset base of the individuals, capturing the true wealth held, rather than the real estate asset portion of wealth. While it may be theoretically appealing, the cost of measuring true wealth and properly adjusting each year, makes a wealth tax very impractical. Measuring wealth at that level would require an extremely high increase in the number of accountants and auditors, all adding cost to the taxation process, and the level of complexity it would add to the legal and tax process is highly impractical. Beyond the logistics, the prior attempted implementations of the asset tax in Europe each led to repeal of these taxes after the targeted wealthy all left their countries rather than wait until their assets were liberated. Germany abolished its wealth tax in 1997, Sweden in 2007 after it became clear that it was driving entrepreneurs out of the country and France abolished its wealth tax in 2017 after 35 Billion Euros of potential investment fled the country in the prior 15 years. Furthermore, the U.S. Constitution prohibits a federal direct tax on asset holdings, in the Fifth Amendment to the Constitution, the Takings Clause. It is the most basic legal protection to private property, preventing the government from deciding that it wants a person's property, preventing a democracy from redistributing the wealth or assets of disfavored groups.

o **The Alternative Minimum Tax** – a proper representation for minors and their families would modify this tax. The tax is designed to prevent high income individuals from eluding taxes legally through use of deductions to reduce net income. It does so through the application of what is effectively a second formula for tax calculation – the taxpayer pays the higher of the two calculations. To be fair to minors and their families, the level of personal exemptions should be substantially increased and account for every family member, so that there is an accurate recognition of the basic cost of living before resources are taxed. The full impact of those personal exemptions should be included before any alternative minimum is calculated to protect the family from the unfair imposition of the alternative minimum. A similar approach is already included in the alternative minimum calculation, by providing different and higher thresholds for married filing jointly or head of household than is received by single filers, but there is no special provision for families. The calculation should also not reduce the value of deductions for all education including private education and training to pursue a professional or personal skill, and not reduce the majority of the deductions related to housing (real estate and mortgage interest) since these correlate to the support and development of minors.

Tax policy demonstrates the effect of the lack of representation of citizens who are minors, since so many significant aspects of tax policy show less consideration of the needs of minors than it would if they were represented. This is the predictable result of the force of the demands of other interest groups taking priority and due to the lack of political power for the young family. Even with the vote, the family will not have the same level of power representative to their size as other more organized, wealthier and more established groups, but the vote will provide some balance. Without better balance, every federal, state and local budget cycle will bring another threat of taxes which impacts the family with minors.

> *Upon the subject of education, not presuming to dictate any plan or system respecting it, I can only say that I view it as the most important subject which we as a people can be engaged in.*
>
> —ABRAHAM LINCOLN
> **March 9, 1832 First Political Announcement**

II EDUCATION POLICY

The first section of this chapter discussed the many areas where government spending and funding policies have an enormous impact on minors and their families and where representation for minors would lead to different policy choices. It also highlighted that many of these policies result in significant and long term effects on minors

– they are not unaffected bystanders. Their lives and futures are greatly influenced by these policy decisions, though they are not represented in the choice of the representatives who make these decisions. This section discusses the second major category of policies that are distorted by the lack of representation of minors, which is in education policy. Minors and their families are obviously the most highly effected by the education policies that are made at the local, state and federal level affecting all tiers of education - primary, secondary and higher education. Despite the central importance of education to their lives, their representation is not comparable to their numbers.

➢ **Primary and Secondary Education** – It can be humbling for Americans to learn for the first time that studies of the academic performance and ability of primary and secondary school U.S. students compared to other countries always shows mediocre performance results.[34] (DESILVER, 2017) The largest global survey administered by the Programme for International Student Assessment which measured science and math literacy at age 15 across 71 countries placed the U.S. number 38 in math and number 24 in science. This is completely consistent with other similar studies. This is partly an indictment of our diminished focus on education and should heighten concern about our education system and the relative neglect for a country of our size and wealth. The nation currently relies heavily on leadership in technology, science and innovation for its economic success and comparative independence from foreign threat. Continued leadership depends on developing its talent internally. It can be supplemented by attracting intelligent, educated and hardworking immigrants, but reliance on H1B visa expansion is not a substitute for a broadly well-educated population of citizens.

It is mostly forgotten that the U.S. once substantially led every nation in the world in its commitment to the education of its citizens. That investment was an important contributor to the rise in the economic and societal improvements in the U.S. throughout the 20th century. By 1850, 80% of children in the relevant age group in the U.S.

were enrolled in primary education, compared to 24% in the United
Kingdom, 37% in Germany, 23% in both Japan and France, and near
0% in China and India. By 1880 the U.S. and France achieved 100%
enrollment, while Germany moved to 50%, U.K. and Japan near 40%,
with India just beginning at 3%. By the end of World War I, the UK
reached 100%, Germany and Japan at 97%, with India still at 12% and
China at 7%. By 1950, both India and China, were still enrolling only
1/3 of children in primary education. Both countries which combined
have 36% of the world's population, continued a sharp climb in enrollment during the next 50 years. By 2000, China achieved 100% and India
reached 92%. India is now at 100%. The United States demonstrated
clear leadership in investing in education, but the time and effects of
that early leadership are passed.[35]

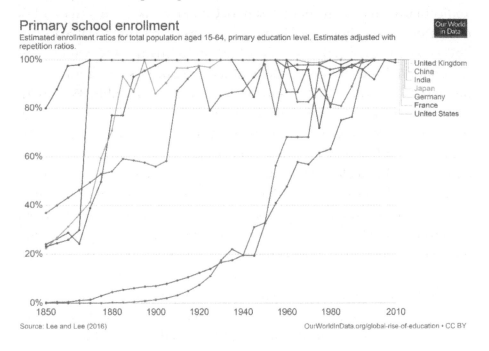

Primary school enrollment

Estimated enrollment ratios for total population aged 15-64, primary education level. Estimates adjusted with repetition ratios.

Source: Lee and Lee (2016)   OurWorldInData.org/global-rise-of-education • CC BY

Public education is the main path into our society for most citizens
raised in the US. It offers the first introduction to extensive peer interaction, cooperation, and competition within a formal organization; it

provides the structured opportunity to develop most of the foundational skills and knowledge that will be used for a lifetime; it allows young citizens to identify their interests and strengths; and it can introduce a path which determines the direction of their lives. Beyond the official and formally structured aspects of public education, the informal aspects also have life changing effects. The interactions with teachers and fellow classmates shape how they perceive the world, their place in the world, and begins to lay the foundation that determines the path of their lives. Values, beliefs, and vocational direction are formed through these interactions.

The importance of education continues to grow as the world continues to progress through the period which is sometimes described as the Information Age. The amount of new information, the use of information, and the ability to access, process and utilize information is rapidly permeating across all human activity. U.S. citizens understand the importance of education and most would like the public system to offer the best education in the world. In the fall of 2016, 50.4 Million students attended public school systems, at a per student cost of $11,600, for a total of $584 Billion. An additional 5.2 M attend private schools, as a better alternative to the free public education system. The public school systems are a massive enterprise and a cost at the same scale as the annual expenditure on national defense – a huge and continuous national investment.

Most of American society supports the belief that devoting time and resources to education is a worthy investment of resources, time, and money. U.S. citizens and thought leaders in business and government repeatedly emphasize that we must improve our education in the STEM subjects (Science, Technology, Engineering and Math) to continue national leadership and innovation in the industries related to the physical and life sciences, medicine, communications, energy, and technology.

The importance of education and the impact of the education system on a child's life is well understood by most parents. For parents with knowledge and choice, many are willing to shoulder great personal sacrifice to send their children to a better school. Nearly 10% of parents carry the extra cost, administration, commuting requirements and often service-to-the-school commitments to forgo the public system, choosing private education as the better alternative. Other parents absorb the additional cost to move to higher priced housing areas and pay the housing premium associated with better performing school districts. Both alternatives, choosing the private school and moving to a better school district, require significant investment by parents.

Unfortunately, many parents are not able to provide the best choice for their children. Many caring parents may believe their children would be better served in a different school, but do not have the flexibility to explore other options. In some situations, parents do not understand the impact of their choices and some simply do not value education sufficiently to be concerned about the options. A child born to a parent who does not have the knowledge, resources, or even inclination to make a true choice may have their potential limited simply because they were condemned to a poorly performing school. This is sad, but true. Limiting a person's potential at such an early time is a problem that should be solved. It is tragic that we allow it to not be solved. But this has been the case for some time, and nothing seems to change. Many initiatives have been launched across the country, each addressing this seemingly intractable problem but none are able to broadly break through. Why?

The problems of underperforming schools have been studied and debated for some time. There is a large academic education establishment dedicated to improving teaching performance, and many worthy initiatives have been underway for quite some time to directly improve the situation, and to experiment and pilot alternatives. But compared to the innovation occurring in life sciences, health care, technology and industry, the progress in education has been poor. The proxy vote proposal does not suggest a specific winning solution but offers a very different approach to solving the problem.

Establishing the proxy vote for minors takes a different approach by dramatically shifting the political influence and power over decisions into the hands of those affected by the decision. It's simply the same process which we use throughout our economy and what we all aspire to across our democratic government and market economy. Corey Booker, U.S. Senator from NJ, and once stellar and reforming Mayor of Newark, NJ, expressed it exceptionally well in a speech delivered in 2012 at a conference of the American Federation for Children:

> *I cannot ever stand up and stand against a parent having options, because I benefited from my parents having options. And when people tell me they're against school choice, whether it's the Opportunity Scholarship Act or charter schools, I look at them and say: "As soon as you're telling me you're willing to send your kid to a failing school in my city, or in Camden or Trenton, then I'll be with you." . . . I am going to fight for the freedom and the liberty and the choice and the options of my people, in the same way you will defend that right for yourself.*

—**COREY BOOKER**

Higher Education Policy The United States is the unrivalled leader in Higher Education. In international rankings of undergraduate, graduate, and professional schools, the United States holds a substantial lead across all major areas. There are several organizations that attempt to rank the quality of institutions and there is some variation that depends on both the chosen ranking criteria and evaluation of that criteria. In each case, the U.S. currently remains unchallenged in leadership. For example, the London based Times Higher Education University Rankings of overall universities in 2018, ranked 17 U.S. universities within the top 25.[36] (Times, 2018) Other rankings show similar results including the QS World University Rankings.[37] (Rankings, 2018) with

14 U.S. universities within the top 25, Shanghai Ranking[38] (Ranking, 2019) [41] with 18 U.S. universities in the top 25, and US News and World Report with 19 U.S. universities in the top 25. The rankings use reasonably objective data, although there may be biases in the assessments, but the U.S. ranks consistently first in a broad range of rankings. The breadth of availability of higher education in the U.S. similarly leads the world, as it does in most specific disciplines.

Higher education viewed as an industry sector is a powerful economic force in the United States. In 2013-14, a total of $517 Billion was spent on higher education, without including the cost of room and board. Total outstanding student debt has climbed to $1.5 Trillion. At the same time, university endowments continue to climb, reaching over $536 Billion in 2013 for the top 830 schools. Endowments can be viewed as the university's savings in the form of investments. Some of the money is earmarked for a specific use, for example for building funds or for funding an endowed Chair which contributes to a professor's compensation. Endowments build through one of three ways: 1) donations by citizens who receive a tax deduction for the donation; 2) through an operating surplus, i.e. tuition, research fees, etc. exceed expenses; and 3) through investment returns on the endowment investments. Unlike average citizens or companies, universities do not pay a tax on the returns on stocks and bonds in their endowment, and as nonprofit and public institutions, are generally tax exempt.[39] (Delisle, 2014)

The 2017 Tax Cuts and Jobs Act changed the tax exemption slightly by establishing a tax on a small minor portion of the net investment income of a small group of the largest endowments. The tax of 1.4 percent will apply to private schools with over 500 students and over $500,000 in endowment per student which the IRS anticipates will affect 25 to 30 of the wealthiest universities in the nation. Since the definitions of net investment income is loose and there are allowances for carve out of assets, it's not yet clear what level of taxation will result. Most citizens would welcome the opportunity to be taxed only 1.4 percent on investment income or any other income. This remains a gaping hole in the nation's tax policies where there is very graduated income tax to capture the income of the wealthiest Americans, but the universities which are equally elite are nearly exempt from taxation. All of that tax advantage is regressive – it is a tax advantage to the wealthy and soon to be wealthy, with no advantage reaching lower income Americans.[40]

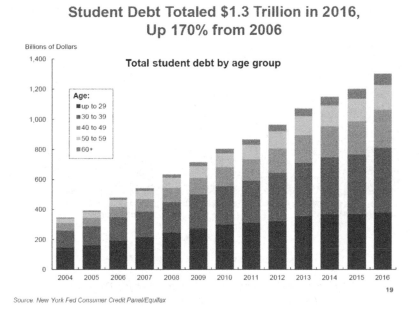

Student Debt Totaled $1.3 Trillion in 2016, Up 170% from 2006

Source: New York Fed Consumer Credit Panel/Equifax

The level of student loan debt has risen high enough to drive longer lasting societal change, some of which creates detrimental secondary effects throughout the economy and throughout our society. Young graduates are delaying marriage as they seek to become less encumbered with debt instead of burdening a new spouse with debt. Some are delaying parenthood and delaying buying a first home as they struggle with the other challenges of job, career, and full adulthood. Others are proceeding with their lives with the extra stress and burden of having debt hanging over them for years. About 40 percent of the student loan debt was used to finance graduate and professional degrees. For those continuing to the graduate or professional education level, the combined undergraduate and graduate debt can be daunting.

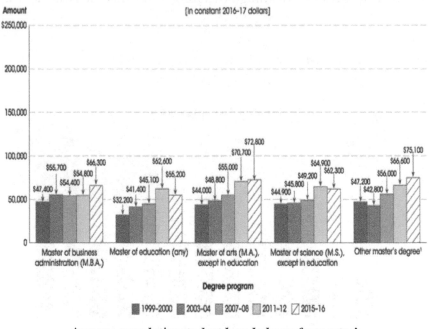

Average cumulative student loan balance for master's degree completers, by degree program.[41]

Most parents would like to assist or cover all of the cost of higher education expenses. However, the choice has become increasingly difficult for many because the costs have increased sufficiently to be out of reach. It has become a choice of digging deeply into retirement savings or letting the burden fall on the young adult.

It has not always been the case that so much national wealth was expended on higher education. For middle class families, there was always the need to make sacrifices for the children who had the opportunity to attend post-secondary education, but the cost increases in tuition and fees have dramatically outpaced family income, overall inflation, housing expenses, and all subcategories of living expense.[42]

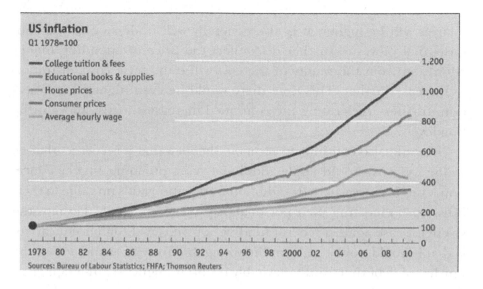

How does this financial aid debt connect to the proxy vote? Does this propose that the proxy will be used to simply vote to wipe the student debt and add it to the ballooning Federal Debt? Or to increase taxes to begin paying for universal higher education paid directly by the federal government? There are strong and simple cases against both of these newly promoted ideas. Wiping the debt is unfair to all of the people who paid for their educations, and to all of the people who did not or could not attend college. It is regressive, since citizens who will receive that benefit are citizens in a position to become wealthier. There is also a strong case against direct federal funding of higher education for many reasons. It would inevitably raise the overall cost of higher education, it would encourage attendance when it doesn't make economic sense to seek the degree, it would be regressive by transferring funds to those likely to be wealthier in the future, and more funds to the more elite among those, and it would be unfair to all the citizens who are going to be carrying the National Debt load.

To repeat the two strongest arguments against this recently proposed new entitlement, many citizens do not plan to attend university so beginning to fund the already advantaged who have the aptitude or desire lacks a normal sense of fairness and is regressive since their later salaries will be higher. It is also generally well understood by economists that moves to further disconnect the price of attending higher education from the reality of the cost will only cause costs of tuition to increase further. This time there would be even higher disconnection, further accelerating the continued increases in cost above inflation levels.

It would also continue to promote the idea that it is correct that *all* young citizens should apply additional years pursuing higher education, even in cases where the additional education adds no value to their lives, nor to meeting their personal or professional goals. Perhaps the strongest case against federal funding for universal higher education, is that it would not be a gift to the young, but instead would add to the burden of debt that would inevitably result. It might be gift-wrapped as wonderful present or entitlement, but the undeniable truth is that the debt will fall upon them and successive generations.

The proxy vote is not a direct solution by itself, but its creation would quickly shift the focus of many legislators to begin to resolve this massive, national problem. There are many interrelated issues and providing a comprehensive proposal is beyond the scale of this book. We know that there are certain pieces of the answer which are known and politically thorny, so are not raised by either party. They are rarely championed by individuals who understand that they would be quickly demonized by powerful opposing forces. Rather than attempt to gingerly step through that minefield, let's scan the field for some simple ideas to spark future consideration.

➢ **Higher Education Cost and Government Policy** – the cost of higher education should be a concern for all citizens, not simply young families. The current outstanding debt load backed by the federal government is $1.6 Trillion, or $5K per U.S. citizen. The debt load carried by students is sufficient to have meaningful and lasting impact on our culture and personally on each individual carrying this debt. Young college graduates increasingly carry debt loads that impose a burden that changes their lives, causing postponement of marriage, delaying having children or buying a first house. Less visible is the personal worry of carrying the heavy burden of a large debt load continuously looming over them. Older American who have experienced the burden of heavy debt can relate to this, while wealthier or less empathetic Americans may not be aware of the impact of this burden. For the young who have less life experience, lower incomes and less security, this level of debt can be truly daunting.

The nation's policies have allowed the higher education system and the financial aid mechanism to create an incredible level of price inflation in higher education over the past 40 years. The current structure creates the environment which encourages universities and colleges to continuously increase prices, extracting the value of their school's brand name from higher income families, and driving middle and lower income families into high levels of debt.

The government has unwittingly fostered the conditions to create this debt. The result has unintentionally created a complicated way to place lower and middle class young adults into a period of something near indentured servitude, forced to work for years to repay loans towards their future; applying all disposable income to repurchase their freedom to pursue their happiness. They can choose to seek the best education available to maximize their future career and earning potential, and then spend the early years of adult life repaying these expenses. Arguably not quite as bad as indentured servitude, since they have some freedom to choose to switch jobs, but the burden of repaying all disposable income towards purchasing their freedom is very similar.

The government is deeply involved in promoting higher education through the structures of the student loan programs and through tax policy. Unfortunately, strategic pricing theory and microeconomic principles suggest that the structure of the student loan programs, and the pricing mechanisms of the universities serve to increase the cost of education and therefore increase the debt levels held by students.

➢ **Price discrimination and the high cost of higher education –** Price discrimination is not illegal and is used increasingly in many industries and businesses to extract the highest price for differences in the ability of customers to pay, and for differences in how different customers value a product or a service, and for small differences between products. The use of price discrimination by higher education institutions is one of the mechanisms that is driving up the cost of education and creates an unfair situation for students and their families as consumers.

Higher education institutions price discriminate by structuring a combination of loans, tuition and fees in a way that lowers the barrier to the student's matriculation, but still maximizes the revenue to the institution. The educational institutions and their supporters state that in this way they are able to assist deserving lower and middle income students to matriculate, but the effect is to assess a willingness to pay and a maximization of the amount received from the student body in an unfair and late in the process communication of the cost of attending any institution. Before proceeding, let's digress to discuss price discrimination and when it is fair vs. unfair.

The most recognizable price discrimination occurs with the airlines, where the same seats are priced differently, and minor differences in where a person is sitting or when a ticket was purchased can mean a huge difference in price. It may sometimes seem unfair that another passenger is receiving a special advantage while waiting for the first class passengers to board, but the likelihood that they paid 3 times the fare for the larger seat, service and convenience, can provide some comfort to most passengers as they walk back to the more confined space of the less expensive seats. That kind of price discrimination is generally accepted as fair and normal and within U.S. societal norms. The same can be said for the better seats at concerts, the theater, sporting events, etc. Price discrimination allows the seller to extract the maximum in total revenue from the sale of goods and services by finding the true market price for each individual and the value of small differences in product or service offerings. It is a fair transaction as long as reasonable price information is provided to the customer. The fact that some citizens are less price sensitive can result in higher profit to the seller or in cases where there is more competition, can supplement the cost to serve some customers.

In cases where there are limited options or where price information is hidden, price discrimination can provide amazing results for the seller, but is clearly unfair to the customer and our society generally seeks to prevent these situations. For a medical example, imagine that you require a life altering surgery. If the surgeon could act as do higher education institutions, they would require a lengthy and difficult process to apply, with submissions from different entities, references, essays, and an extensive, detailed life history. Shortly before you must make a life altering decision, you must then provide detailed financial information to assess various items that will determine the price. Late in the process, with time running out, or on your way into the operating room, the surgeon then provides you with a price which is far more money than you are accustomed to evaluating. In the medical case, think of it as a life altering surgery that is needed soon or nearly immediately, just as the college decision is to young applicants.

This is comparable to the experience of prospective students when facing the daunting task of meeting college tuition and traversing the many layers of grants and loans that the schools, government, and other agencies provide. Few students pay the list price, and the decisions on the final price are made late in the game after a huge commitment by the students and leaving limited time for decision making. As an alternative example, imagine that after you buy a home or move into an apartment, the water and electric company, and the real estate taxing authority require that you provide extensive financial information before they decide what your rates will be. Both examples are analogous to the pricing discrimination exercised by universities. There is a steep and time-consuming application process, requiring extensive effort by students, often with many prior years of emotional and financial support from their parents. The choice of school is a life altering decision. Students must devote years of preparation, followed by an extensive and complex application process towards multiple schools while feeling time pressure throughout the process.

At the end of that difficult process, lurks a financial aid process which is a wolf in sheep's clothing. Extensive financial information is gathered from parents and students, with the stated purpose of assisting students with aid. However, the less apparent objective is to support efforts to be effective in price discriminating between students, combining grants and aid to ensure that the school meets various quality targets for the incoming class, while maximizing tuition revenue.

In this case, price discrimination is completely unfair. Higher education is allowed far too much latitude to discriminate between individuals, demanding extensive insight into a family's resources to decide how to price to them. Since fully two thirds of students receive financial aid, it's clear that this has become a pricing game, rather than simply assistance for low-income students. That discrimination is one of several combined factors that drives up the cost for everyone. Universities act as businesses, spending large sums on marketing and administration to drive demand, building the brand to pump up the willingness to pay, and then extracting that value from each individual family. One major step towards reducing this upward vicious cycle is to prevent this level of price discrimination – there should be a reference price and nearly everyone pays that price, with the only exceptions being for needs-based scholarships or academic performance that is objectively distinctly different than peer applicants. Most businesses must hold to that same standard of fairness. There is no reason for universities to receive this kind of royal power, beyond some historic cultural deference to the educated elite.

➤ **Student Loan Debt and the Academy** - There are good societal and macroeconomic reasons for the government to support financial aid through loan guarantees to encourage higher education. But while aid supports the student and their families to pursue their goals of an education, that same aid later can become a burden to the former student and their families. A better balance is needed to ensure that when the support is provided, it is actually likely to be beneficial to the life of that citizen.

This support has failed when the result for students is to provide an education that costs more than they can afford. Default rates have reached 11.3 percent for public colleges and 7.4 percent for private.[43] (Douglas-Gabriel, 2017) Part of this problem stems from the lack of 'skin in the game' for the universities and colleges in ensuring that the value they provide towards the future success of their former students is worth the cost. The consequent defaults are an objective measure of their success. While the default rates have some importance to schools, the importance of those rates is not on a scale to match the cost. The negative impact of the defaults is only felt by the institutions with the most egregious level of defaults. The Department of Education can impose sanctions on institutions that exceed a 40 percent default rate in a single year or 30 percent for 3 consecutive years. Imagine a bank continuing to lend with these default rates! Without a more direct connection to the cost of default and the results in employability outcomes, it is easy for the universities and colleges to lose the connection to their role of preparing the students for a viable future.

To be fair to all citizens, including those who do not receive the benefit of higher education or aid, the institution must become more directly responsible for the defaults which must be tracked and applied to each institution. The responsibility for the cost of defaults should not be assigned to the general population of citizens, but rather to the schools that admit or graduate or do not graduate those who are later unable to pay. This may result in colleges being forced to reduce cost, or eliminate programs that do not lead to educating students for a productive future. Ideally, it will lead to increased efforts to educate in order to create a more productive citizen. For some institutions that do not seek to educate towards employability, it may require more fund raising from donors who support their more general mission.

The mission of higher education is not solely to prepare students for a viable and financially sound future. It can be a blend of preparation and enrichment and can be directed solely towards enriching the student's inner life and pursuit of happiness. However, the pursuit of knowledge towards the general pursuit of happiness should not be the responsibility of all U.S. taxpayers, in the same way that a citizen pursuing happiness through a Hawaii vacation or through excellent physical fitness, should not expect fellow citizens to finance that pursuit. The government should not attempt to decide the proper balance between general enrichment and preparation for a viable future. A free market approach can solve that problem by allowing the market to decide by simply charging defaults to the institution. Colleges and universities should be the ones on the hook for defaulted loans for general pursuit of happiness, not average American citizens who have nothing to do with this choice and this system.

The higher education institutions that seek to fund many students who graduate with insufficient skills or who fund students that lack desire or interest to work in roles which support repaying the debt, will require greater outside funding or lower costs to offset the default rates. It will require greater focus on raising funds from individuals and foundations who support the need and value of that program and pursuit as worthwhile. Or the institutions may determine a mix of students with defaulting and non-defaulting pursuits. While this might shift the mission and focus of some universities, some may find that preparing their graduating students and young alumni for employment and supporting longer term career placement doesn't require a negative shift to their broad mission.

This approach should support future innovation by encouraging experimental approaches to higher education. For example, some will develop programs which allow students who want to explore general ideas, or more esoteric knowledge to use lower cost processes and therefore at lower tuition or do so in the same way as the general population - in their spare time. A free market approach will allow this to adjust more sustainably and naturally. The benefits to students will be that it will reduce the excessive number of degrees which do not offer economic or societal value, beyond what can be achieved in high school. Universities will get closer to the important goal of preparing students for the challenges ahead and reduce focus on simply attracting more students to campus. This will be good for all citizens.

➤ **Tax advantages for donations** - Hidden among the many tax benefits which are given to universities are the tax deductions for donations to higher education institutions. In 2017, $43.6 Billion was donated to higher-education institutions.[44] (Joselyn, 2018) Since nearly all of these donations were leveraging a tax deduction, the U.S. government is participating in the donations to these institutions by foregoing what would otherwise have been taxable income. As a result, college endowments at some universities have grown so large that the private investment fund side of many universities is beginning to dwarf the academic side. The structure of these tax benefits does not require reducing tuition and making it more affordable for students, and without that, is not necessarily a benefit to the current student population. This deduction is also a benefit from the general population of Americans to the university, though the vast majority will not attend these universities.

Tax deductions for funds that will directly support tuition payment of students is more understandable as a general good for the nation, though it is again a benefit to the more elite group of Americans. In contrast, tax deductions for growing the prestige and power of the school by building gold-plated gyms named for the donating alum, or funding a large sports team staff, or promoting the general views of university professors or leaders do not provide a benefit to the nation and simply create competition between schools for students and faculties. High salaries for its leaders, large pension plans, a large balance sheet of funds, private residences for select university leaders – this is like old style wasteful private corporations from another era. All of these spoils would be less of a problem if it were not funded by government financial aid and the tax deductions for donations.

An example of this warping effect of the tax deduction can be seen by looking at the value of endowments. For example, the Harvard Endowment had grown to $37.1 Billion by 2017, or over $1.8 Million dollars for every student currently attending Harvard. Unquestionably, there are sufficient funds that no student would need to pay tuition. There is no question that a Harvard education is highly valued and in high demand, so there is no need to discount their tuition, nor, presumably, are there many student loan defaults coming from Harvard alums. But there is a question about giving tax benefits to wealthy Harvard alums and friends of Harvard for donating simply to continue to build the prestige of the school. It is the free choice of the donors to donate and this should not be changed, but unless the money is applied directly to scholarships for needy students, providing the deduction redistributes the need for taxes to other citizens, while providing secondary benefits to the alum including prestige, sports tickets, legacy admissions influence, and many other benefits.

➤ **Tax policy of Higher Education Costs** – The one benefit that should be retained and expanded is some form of deduction for higher education costs. Repayment of financial aid should be completely deductible against a person's future income tax in the same way that an individual's capital losses can be written against gains. The reasoning is simple – until the student has achieved the breakeven point on their investment in education, it is not fair to begin taxing them on that investment. This would be consistent with many other treatments of investment, specifically how capital investment is treated in the accounting for capital gains, how operating expenses and losses are written off against revenue and how they are accounted for across tax years. This would also provide the young a more fair tax burden in their early years as they struggle to get established.

➢ **Monopolistic Policies in College Sports** – This issue is placed last since the impact on the overall population is small, but it has a very large effect on the lives of those affected. It is another example of an unfair situation which disadvantages the young and their families because their influence and political power is insufficient to overcome the embedded political power. College sports is a national-scale business, comparable in economic power to the largest professional sports organizations. Yet college sports have continued to enforce policies that prevent compensating athletes. When the issue is debated, it is usually framed with the example of the superstar athlete, one who will make a king's fortune in a couple of years of professional play. However, the fact is that an average of only 1.5% of Division 1 college football and men's college basketball ever play on a professional team, with many of those having a very short career.

Whether an athlete will one day earn a fortune should not enter into the evaluation of what is correct and fair but imagining that a large number of these athletes are being positioned for high lucrative salaries creates a bias which prevents the issue from receiving a fair evaluation. It is hard to create energy around short term financial fairness when we believe those students will all become superstar professional athletes, so it is important that this be considered with facts and quantifiable data, rather than anecdata.

The two most financially lucrative college sports by far, Men's Football and Basketball, have every characteristic of a large and wealthy professional business. According to a 2016 USA today summary of the top 230 NCAA Division I public schools, the athletic departments generated $9.7 Billion in revenue with $9.4 Billion in costs.[45] (Kelly, 2018) This does not include the private schools which are not required to disclose financial results, therefore excluding highly valuable programs like Notre Dame, Miami, USC, Syracuse, Stanford, Duke, and many others. It also does not include smaller schools; nor does this include the less measurable but very important value benefit that the schools receive through attracting student applications and matriculation because of their sports reputation; nor the additional donations to the school from alumni and fans which are an associated benefit of the brand building effect of prominent college teams. That $9.7 Billion in college sports compares to $13 Billion for the NFL in 2016, and $4.8 Billion for the NBA;[46] (Kutz, 2016) so the combination across all college sports at these schools delivers around 55% of the combined revenue of professional football and basketball. Though not the same value, it is fair to state that college sports is financially a very valuable business.

So, if this were a normal market economy business like professional sports, how much would players be paid? The other side of that question - if this were not a monopoly and the players could receive compensation, how much would that be? There is no single and conclusive way to state how much players would be paid if the payment restriction were removed. However, here are some comparisons which offer a good sense of proportion:

- **Coach Compensation** – Compensation for top college coaches is nearly the same as for professionals. For coaches, it is reasonable to believe that they are paid this way for economically sound reasons. The financial value they provide is worth attracting the best talent in a free market for coaches. The top 10 highest paid college coaches in 2016 received $64M in salary, or $6.4M each, not including endorsements and other income, quite comparable to the top 10 coaches among the NFL which is $69M. Here compensation is very similar and within 10%. The workload for the college and professional coaches are similar, with professionals facing a longer season, with 16 vs. 12 regular season games, 4 pre-season games, and 4 playoff rounds. Both groups of coaches are at the top of their fields and each have significant management challenges which are different but arguably comparable in terms for expertise needed.
- **Revenue per player** - The NFL revenue per player was $5.4 Million, player compensation absorbing approximately 57%

of all football revenue, therefore $3.1M in compensation per athlete. In the NBA, the finances are different, with smaller facilities but a higher number of games, and smaller teams, yielding a higher revenue per athlete at $10.6M and $6.1M per athlete in compensation. To assess how revenue per athlete would compare to colleges, the same revenue per player approach can be used to size what the equivalent would be for college players in an open market. Take the 30 teams in the NBA and the 32 teams in the NFL and compare them to the top 31 schools, therefore 62 teams, which report revenue (since each school has a football and basketball program). For that top 31 schools, the revenue per player is $1.3 Million; by applying the same 57% compensation per revenue dollar, used for NFL and NBA, the result would be an average athlete compensation at $750,000 per year. These revenue numbers include other sports, including women's basketball, baseball, track, and the data was not available to extract that revenue, but even the high estimate of 20% applied to those, still results in $600,000 per athlete.

For many of these athletes, that $600,000 per athlete may be the peak of their lifetime earning potential since only 1.5% of college football and 1.1 % of men's college basketball players ever play at the professional level.[47] (NCAA Recruiting Fact Sheet, 2018)[48] (Patrick Gleeson, 2018) (It is fair to argue that the top 31 college teams will have higher success rates in developing players who become professionals, but this does not diminish the fairness point of the argument.) In a free and open market, these students would be paid a substantial salary. The suggestion that tuition and other student perks are a fair alternative to $600,000 is clearly not valid - something of a head fake actually - since the vast majority of division 1 athletes in top football and basketball programs must greatly neglect their studies to devote time to the sport.

* **Racial mix of teams** - The NFL and NBA both have a disproportionally high level of African-American athletes, with 69%[49] and 74%. (Perry, 2015) (Sports Business News, 2016) Of the total student body, African-American males make up 15% of college age males and represent 38% of college football athletes, 45% of college basketball athletes, 20% of track athletes, and 6% of the athletes in all of the other remaining college sports.[50] (NCAA, 2017) African-American athletes are most highly represented, disproportional to their relative concentration in the overall population and within the college student body, in exactly the sports where there would be the highest potential for significant salaries. It should be disturbing to every American that these statistics indicate that African-American men, a historically economically and politically disadvantaged group, are highly represented in this group that is responsible for the revenue through their contributions on the playing field and court, but who are not receiving compensation. Stated simply, black male athletes are highly represented in this group that is being unfairly restricted from an open market wage for their participation in a very lucrative business. Is this reminiscent of something? It is shocking that universities filled with professors teaching and researching on a host of social justice issues do not directly protest this dubious practice in their own backyard.

* **Scholarships and Financial Aid** – The schools are widely distributing scholarships and financial aid. For example, a survey of 352 Division I schools indicated that $2.2B in athletic scholarships and another $2.2 Billion in other financial aid was being disbursed. The money is not going to the athletes who earn it for the revenue producing sports. Only $0.7B of the $2.2B or 36% of the scholarship money is distributed to football and men's basketball with the other scholarship money distributed to supporting all of the other teams.[51] (ScholarshipStats.org, 2017) Since African-American men are underrepresented on the other

teams and have higher representation on the money producing teams, this is another redistribution of wealth from the historically economically disadvantaged to the advantaged group.

This issue of fairness has been festering for some time. The former UCLA basketball star and MVP of the 1995 NCAA Basketball Tournament, Ed O'Bannon, along with other former players, filed a lawsuit against the NCAA in 2009 claiming violations of the Sherman Antitrust Act, seeking compensation for the commercial use of their names and images in video games and archival recordings. Judge Wilken ruled that the NCAA's practice of barring payments to athletes violated antitrust laws and ordered that schools should be permitted to offer full cost-of-attendance scholarships to athletes, covering all cost-of-living expenses that were not currently part of NCAA scholarships, and that colleges should be permitted to place as much as $5,000 into a trust for each athlete per year of eligibility. This would have at least been a step in the right direction. However, the NCAA appealed, and the ruling was overturned arguing that Wilken did not properly consider the 1984 Supreme Court case, NCAA v. Board of Regents of the University of Oklahoma. In that case the NCAA was denied control of college football television rights, (meaning that the schools could control television rights – which didn't do anything to pay players) and the court found that: "To preserve the character and quality of the 'product,' athletes must not be paid." The court ruled against the association, saying its amateurism rule violated the antitrust laws. But the court went on to say that the association may restrict colleges from compensating athletes beyond offering scholarships and a few thousand dollars for "the cost of attendance." In September of 2016, the Supreme Court declined to hear any appeal.

The finding defies logic and the financial evidence. Although universities may claim that paying the athletes would taint the purity of the game, it's clear that college sports, certainly the big money games of men's football and basketball, have been highly professional in every sense of the word, for quite some time. They have everything that wealthy and successful public companies aspire to, including large highly compensated staff, impressive state-of-the-art training facilities and stadiums, professional recruiting staff, public relations professionals, marketing departments, travel planners, impressive television coverage with multiyear deals, marketing and branding deals, and a broadcasting network, ESPN, which relies heavily on their programming for much of the year. There is an entire professionally managed organization, the NCAA, with a billion dollars of annual revenue in 2018 to plan their activities and protect the barrier to paying players. If all college sports were truly amateur, the ticket prices would not be so high, there would not be quite so much value in marketing the images, and there would not be coaches paid comparable to those of professional sports. Some honesty and justice would be good to see here. It is not fair to the young athletes to continue in this way.

The NCAA should be prevented from continuing this cartel and allow a free market to exist. They should be prevented from organizing the collusion between schools that prevents paying free citizens for their labor. Each school can then decide whether it wants to field a scholarship-only team, a paid team or a mixed team and do its best to attract the best players, just as is done in other situations in any free and open market. Some schools may continue to not pay and use the money to fund other sports or academic activity, and others may choose to pay their players and fully fund their athletic programs. Each choice is fine as long as there is no collusion to decide. It is the collusion, anti-competitive behavior, and monopolist activity that is wrong. There is nothing wrong with a school fielding an all-volunteer or scholarship-only squad, and it will be interesting to observe the teams play. Separate leagues may emerge, a volunteer or scholarship-only league, and a paid league. Let the free market decide.

The fact that we are taking hard earned money from young African-American men and women, some who may be at the peak of their earning power, should disturb us all. We've all seen the newspaper story about a past star player who is in a low paying job in their middle age, after delivering so much entertainment to their fans and honor to their school as a college player. The low paying job is not the sad thing here, it is that the player does not have the nest egg that they earned as a young athlete. Someone else is walking around with that money.

The best evidence that there is enough money to pay them? Here it is: there is enough money for a highly compensated NCAA executive team, for highly compensated coaches and staffs, for gold plated gyms dedicated to teams, and for highly compensated university administrations. So, there must be money for players. Simply allow it to be an open market, and some players will receive little compensation, and some will receive high compensation, just as in the rest of society. Allow pay for the contribution of the players and stop criminalizing young athletes and their families for accepting free dinners from agents and for selling their sneakers to make a few dollars.

III IMMIGRATION POLICY

The number of undocumented immigrants living in the U.S. in 2014 is estimated at 12.1 Million people.[52] (Baker, 2014) This is not a small number, and equivalent to having entire nations embedded within the US, all living in hiding, without full legal protections, and without representation. For a sense of scale, here are entire nations which are comparable in size: Cuba 11.5M, Bolivia 11.0 M, Haiti 11.0M, Dominican Republic 10.8 M, Belgium 11.4M, Greece 11.2M, Czech Republic 10.6M, Portugal 10.3M, Sweden 9.9M, or Hungary 9.7M. Within that undocumented group, the subset who emigrated from the regions of Mexico and Central America is a total 7.9M of the 12.1M,[53] (Institute, 2016) roughly two thirds. That group is comparable to the entire nations of Austria 8.7M, Switzerland 8.5M, Israel 8.3M, Bulgaria 7.1M, Laos 6.8M, Paraguay 6.8 M, El Salvador 6.4M, Libya 6.4 M, or Nicaragua 6.2M, or the combination of Puerto Rico 3.7M and Uruguay 3.5M. According to the Department of Homeland Security, 75 percent of these undocu-mented immigrants have lived in the United States for over 10 years, so are established and would have been eligible to become American citi-zens some time ago except for the important issue of their entry process to the U.S. According to the Department of Homeland Security, the level of increase in the number of total undocumented immigrants has reduced to 125,000 per year for the years between 2010 and 2014. That is a reduction from 500K per year between 1990 and 2007. The 125k per year is the equivalent of 2400 people per week, or 2 loaded 727's per day – a large amount of people seeking ways to overcome high barriers to become citizens. Apprehensions at the border remain very high at 303,000 in 2017 at the Southwest border or 5800 per week or the equiva-lent of 6 loaded 727's per day in apprehensions. In 2019, these numbers have increased with the Border Patrol apprehending 132K migrants attempting to cross the Southwest border in May 2019. American citizen-ship is valuable and many of these undocumented citizens are coming from desperate situations. The combination of the value of citizenship and the poor and often violent conditions in home countries is suffi-cient to overcome the requirement to risk life and detention to cross the border and willingly live a life without citizen's rights.

Immigration policy affects minors more than any other demo-graphic group. There are two obvious reasons: 1. Immigration has a very long-term cycle of impact on the nation, and minors have the longest number of years remaining as citizens. Obviously, the average child with 75 years of remaining life expectancy will have a future life experience that is affected by immigration decisions made today. On the other hand, someone with a life expectancy of 1 or 15 years is less liable to be affected directly. The second reason is that young families are more apt to share government resources, like schools and hospitals, with undocumented immigrants, and are more likely to live in close proximity to immigrants than would those in the middle to later age groups, the wealthy and elite, or young singles. Documented and legally entering immigrants are more highly educated and middle to upper economic class, with better English language skills, and they too are more likely to share resources with young families.

The fact that immigrants effect minors and their families more than other citizens is not an argument to increase or decrease the number of documented or undocumented immigrants, it is simply an important consideration which relates to the proxy vote. In fact, there is no data to indicate how their parents would vote regarding undocumented immigrants or on expanding the number of annual legal immigration. Data is also unavailable to prove the point made in the discussion above about the level of contact and use of resources, but it seems sufficiently obvious to be included. The longevity point is numerically true without further proof, so no supporting data is necessary. It is clear, though, that the older, wealthy, Hollywood producer or High-Tech executive who argues for increasing immigration or criticizes the mission of the Immigration and Customs Enforcement Agency (ICE) does not have real "skin in the game". The immigrant will not be competing with that executive for a job, not living as an equal in that person's community, or sharing schools with their children. The Hollywood producer may perhaps even get the benefit of lower landscaping, food or restaurant costs since undocumented immigrants often must accept the most labor-intensive jobs, often underpaid or paid under the table, off the grid and living without civil rights. The tech executive may receive the benefit of access to more skilled workers locally but may not directly absorb other longer term impact. Similarly, the older wealthy nativist who wants to end all immigration may also have little real contact with immigrants and little "skin in the game" over the long term and may have other motives for their preferences. They have the right to their opinions and the right to choose representatives to promote their views. But most affected are minors and their families - the ones that are underrepresented.

This relatively high impact on the lives of minors is the primary immigration-related argument for representation of minors through a vote. This discussion does not attempt to suggest any broad solutions beyond providing a voice to minor citizens and their families by establishing the proxy vote. There are many issues that prevent a resolution to the current stalemate between the political parties, and between viewpoints among Americans, which are beyond the scope of this discussion. However, there are two other points related to immigration that are relevant.

First, the United States provides for a transition for immigrants towards citizenship which allows a spouse of a U.S. Citizen to become a citizen after three years; for a green card holder the period is five years. They can then hold dual citizenship with U.S. voting rights, along with their prior nationality. That seems fair and reasonable enough; however, a native U.S. born minor must wait 18 years for their fair representation, so 13 years or 3 Presidential election cycles longer than the immigrant who may have dual loyalties and retain a different history and values. Comparatively, that does not seem fair and provides an immigrant with a priority in representation over a native born U.S. citizen.

The second point is simply that the immigration problem falls heavily on minors and their families. The status quo provides for exactly what Americans abhor - the creation of a lower caste or peasant class of people living in the nation without equal rights. This group of undocumented immigrants is aspiring to a better life and often choose to pay their savings to 'coyotes" to help them enter the country illegally. Forced to live in hiding, with limited civil rights, their lives are forever scarred by our representatives' inability to reach a reasonable solution to an internal political disagreement. The nation's children are forced to observe our ineffectual efforts at enforcing borders and what seems a lack of real compassion to those in need. The effect of the new votes from the proxy could lead to clearing the bottleneck by shifting more conscience and effort into resolving these issues.

IV NATIONAL SECURITY

National security and defense are among the most important functions of all national governments and is the highest government expenditure category in the U.S. outside Social Security and Medicare. Defending the nation and the nation's allies against invaders is in the shared interest of all citizens and is an existential requirement. Defense is always financially costly for obvious reasons, but the highest personal cost is always born by the young. Historically, nations turn to some level of conscription in times of war with the burden inevitably falling primarily on the young to do the fighting, those who are just leaving the ranks of minors. Beyond the soldiers themselves, there is a personal impact on the young families of the soldiers. The U.S. ended conscription in 1973, but in the years immediately preceding, during the Vietnam War, the draft included young men ages 18 to 26,[54](Wikipedia) drafting 2.2 Million military personnel between 1965 and 1972. Even without the draft, front line soldiers will tend to be young. It is a very different thing to support a military action when it is abstract to you as an individual, than when it is you or your child that is about to ship to foreign soil, possibly never to return. If parents had a proxy vote, only in cases of true national need, would a nation be willing to make the commitment of boots on the ground. The focus would shift to methods of projecting power through alternative means and capabilities, to avoid loss of life.

One could fear that establishing the proxy vote for minors might create too pacifist or isolationist a nation, one that would not be sufficiently courageous to defend itself. But parents of minors should not be expected to assess all actions through a warped lens of fear. More probably the contrary will be true. Rather than allow the nation to become weak, they would support greater strength through technology, investment, and skill to avoid wasting precious human life. A professional military, well-funded with investment to achieve clear and overwhelming technological leadership can save lives and support a better defense. Combined with a population of citizens that are seeking neither expansion nor conflict, it should be an even more stabilizing force for the world. The same issues and debate over national security will be advanced, but one should expect a different set of tradeoffs with an even higher value placed on human life. The difference is that the proxy voters would be more highly concerned about casualties than the average voter, supporting higher emphasis on spending for better military technology to preserve human life. It might also increase willingness to support troops and veterans and those willing to serve in the armed forces, to prevent the need for future conscription. The most important shift, however, is a more sober respect for when and how to use troops and technology.

Another change in national defense policies that may be encouraged through the proxy, is a shift towards younger government representatives, who may then influence a more modern outlook on national defense. U.S. government leaders have been slow to understand the speed with which technology is creating significant threats to the nation. Some of this is attributable to the age and backgrounds of the representatives, who are selected because they reflect the issues of concern to an older population. These older citizens tend to be later adopters of new technology, and less in tune with the level of change. The average age of members of Congress is 61 for Democrats and 57 for Republicans, with professional experience skewed to law, politics and business. Beyond the need for younger representatives, there is a need for a higher representation of other professional disciplines including technology, medicine, and physical sciences to deal with the defense and healthcare challenges of the future.

The threats of cyberwarfare and cyberterrorism and the potential to attack the banking systems and electric grid are real future threats, and the U.S. is moving at slower speed than it should when considering the potential for catastrophic events in these areas. It would be easy to argue that we should already have formed a fully resourced Cyber warfare force with defensive and offensive capability, as an equal branch of the armed forces. We know we have been attacked by North Korean, Chinese, Iranian and Russian hackers in the past, with little sign that their governments will stop the hackers, and there is real potential that these governments are behind the attacks. We should be able to both defend and attack as necessary. The nation has capabilities in the intelligence services, defense department, and within corporations, but it is not nearly at the scale of the threat that these challenges present now, and well short of the scale to handle the threats that the future may present. The proxy will be an enabler to resolve this, but the nation should not wait for that long cycle process for establishing the vote to deal with these issues.

VI AMERICAN CULTURE

This discussion of culture refers to the use of the word "culture" as the attitudes, behaviors, and beliefs that are characteristic within a group, not the more limited reflection seen through the arts, which is also referred to as culture. American culture encompasses many subcultures, with differences that cut along geographic, economic, ethnic, racial, social class, educational, or personal interest differences. Members of a subculture are not predetermined through their personal character-istics or interests, but more often as a matter of choice to embrace the preferences and stereotypes that align one fully to a subculture. Within these many differences, there are common threads of belief and behav-ior that can be referred to as American Culture, though it is difficult to actually define American Culture.

American culture is in a state of continuous change. The pace of change has been accelerated by the establishment and proliferation of mass media over the past century, by the introduction of com-puter technology over the past 50 years, the internet over the past 25 years, and finally over the past 10 years through the introduction of personal communications devices and social media. This is bound to continue into the future. The interaction and personal develop-ment and contributions of 330 Million people in the U.S., along with the over 7.5 Billion in the rest of the world, combined with the development of innumerable different paths of technological inno-vation guarantees that change will continue and possibly continue to accelerate.

Information and communications technology has been an important driver of the changes in American culture, but the longer waves of change to the culture have been driven by the expansion of the vote, first to some minority groups, then to women and later to all minority groups and finally to full enforcement of these rights. The enforcement of voting rights was an essential step in moving the government towards full equal rights under the law. These changes are still relatively new, and the nation remains in a state of change, but remaining faithful to the constitution and the nation's laws continues to press society towards that goal of equality.

The vote itself creates a much broader influence than the impact on the government through the selection of representatives. In the same way that government representatives recognize the shift in power and priorities when the group of constituents changes, so do all of the other organizations within the nation. From corporations to single issue interest groups, there is a shift in platform to adjust to the shift in voting power when there is a new center of gravity for society as a whole. That shift in focus then echoes throughout society, across corporations, the media, etc. until all participants eventually adjust themselves to the new reality. These changes have had a dramatic impact on the improvement of the quality of life for minorities and women in America. A very different but also very important combination of improvements would come from the implementation of the proxy vote for minors. These would affect Americans at the very beginning of their lives, when so much of the course of their future is determined. It could transform the entire society in ways that we cannot foresee, but we can have confidence that it would create a more welcoming world for the generations that follow.

1) American Culture: Media and minors

During the emergence of early mass media – radio, movies, television, newspapers and magazines – there were both legal and informal strictures on the levels of violence, profanity, sexuality and what was then called depravity. The restrictions were in line with the general beliefs of the majority of the American public and reflective of the culture. Beginning in the late 1950's, the rules and the culture began to change. In 1957 with Butler vs. State of Michigan, the courts overturned a Michigan statute which outlawed printed material containing obscene language, finding the wording of the restriction, "tending to the corruption of the morals of youth," was too broad: "The State insists that, by thus quarantining the general reading public against books not too rugged for grown men and women in order to shield juvenile innocence, it is exercising its power to promote the general welfare. Surely, this is to burn the house to roast the pig."[55] (Frontline)

There have been several court cases since that time, which apply the First Amendment rights and the concept of community standards that will prevent the likelihood that the proxy vote would lead to excessive censorship. However, there may be more thoughtful emphasis and application of those standards to protect the young and innocent, when many of the ideas and images which may be acceptable to most adults, are an obvious assault to a young developing mind.

This discussion is not intending to promote censorship, nor will it wade into a study of the impact of violent games and offensive language on young minds. Most parents, guardians, and psychologists agree that the level of violence and profane images which are directly and openly marketed to minors has stepped beyond a reasonable line. Some responsible and enforced standards seem reasonable without the need to prevent adults from access to adult materials.

2) American Culture: The Culture Wars

The term culture war refers to the polarization and struggle between often directly opposing values and views about nearly everything in public and private life; government, language, human relationships, etiquette, the environment, basic values, interests, personal choice, law, manners, freedom, history, and a long list of other categories that have been major battlegrounds. The list seems to be expanding, rather than converging towards common views. It reaches deeply into the nation's legal choices, definitions of freedom, the meaning and enforcement of the Constitution, and down into the way that people choose or are permitted to interact. The battleground is vast, with some of the largest battles settled in the courts. There are daily skirmishes, some staged and financed by hidden groups, covered by the media, each side with their own coverage. The direction and speed of culture change can only be influenced, not decided, since the inputs and changes are not predictable, nor easily controlled.

The culture wars are fueled by strongly held beliefs that there is an optimal and right set of choices on many topics, and the balance of power will continue to ebb and flow on different issues. As citizens change and develop individually, so will the views of the citizenry as a whole. Interpretation of law and freedoms by the judiciary will sometimes outweigh the beliefs of the citizenry, and that is part of the system.

The proxy vote will affect this only by improving the representation of the interests of young citizens. Many of the past, current, and likely the future battles in the culture wars will have a very direct and immediate impact on minors and their families, and certainly have long lasting effect. Without a vote, their interests are not properly represented within the governmental battles and indirectly through the choice of the judiciary. Minors and their families will always be disadvantaged compared to other powerful groups leading the culture wars, since they lack the financial and experience advantages of older citizens and more militant single issue childfree adults, but the proxy vote would at least allow some additional representation in the government that will bring them closer to a position of power equal to their numbers.

3) American Culture: The War on Drugs

The term "The War on Drugs" was first popularized after a speech by Richard Nixon in 1971, which declared drug abuse "public enemy number one". The Comprehensive Drug Abuse Prevention and Control

Act of 1970 was consistent with the prohibitions enacted earlier and included some additional reporting requirements for pharmaceutical industry record keeping and some flexibility in mandatory sentencing. Nearly 50 years later, drug abuse in the U.S. is much worse as evidenced by all relevant measures. The number and rates of death by overdose, the proliferation of alternative forms of narcotics, the number of people jailed, the power and reach of the established drug cartels, now operating from narco-states and narco-economies, and the terror they have created in their own nations are all evidence that the situation is continuing to deteriorate.[56]

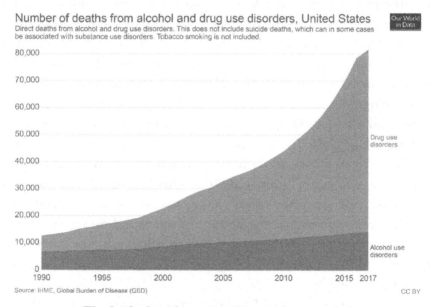

Number of deaths from alcohol and drug use disorders, United States

Direct deaths from alcohol and drug use disorders. This does not include suicide deaths, which can in some cases be associated with substance use disorders. Tobacco smoking is not included.

Source: IHME, Global Burden of Disease (GBD)

CC BY

The deaths from drug use continue to increase much
more quickly than growth in population.

The nation has begun treating marijuana differently than the more dangerous drugs. Some states have moved towards legalization, most for medical use, and several for taking the steps to legalize for recreational use. Since marijuana remains illegal in Federal law, U.S. citizens do take a risk of an arrest under federal law.

How does the Proxy vote effect this issue and the results?

During election cycles, there is often some reference to drugs, crime, and incarceration rates. The Democrats and Republicans state differences in approach which reflect their beliefs, biases, and the opinions of the preferences of their constituencies. However, it is largely correct that, beyond marijuana legislation, there has been very limited difference in their prioritization of the issues. For the leading political parties this issue is dangerous and far from the core of their message. For the many families who have been touched by the impact of drugs directly or through the drug war happening in the nearby community, this is the primary issue which effects their lives. Most parents begin to understand the level of threat posed beginning in their child's preteen years and that can remain a concern through adulthood. This concern crosses all boundaries - economic, race, ethnicity, class, and region. With the new emergence of the opioid epidemic, we now have a drug that is being adopted later in life, so that new members of our families are under threat. Drug overdose deaths in the U.S. have risen to a shocking total of 70,000[57] (Statistics) reported deaths for the 12 months preceding January 2018. It has been increasing year over year with only recent signs of stabilizing by mid-2019. This is a very high number of people suffering an unnecessary death, but one should consider that much higher numbers are affected in the surrounding family which is gravely suffering due to that death. Add to this the high numbers who suffer from addiction, or who suffer due to a criminal record associated with drug use or sale.

To provide perspective of the comparative size of the 70,000 lives lost to overdose in a single year – over the 20 years of the Vietnam War, the U.S. lost 47,424 brave women and men in combat and another 10,785 from other non-combat causes for a total of 58,209.[58] (Wikepedia) Since 1980, the U.S. has suffered less than 8,000 total deaths across all military operations. The 70,000 lost to drug overdose in a single year is nearly 9 times the number of our military deaths over the last 40 years. This comparison should not be seen to in any way diminish the noble sacrifice of military personnel who lay down their lives in service of the nation. It is used here only to point to the huge size of tragic loss that we are repeating every year, without addressing the drug problem with the urgency of a true national emergency.

Beyond drug overdose deaths, there are a comparably large set of issues surrounding violence and criminality fostered by the attempt to stem the flow of drugs and a large prison population due to drug related crime. Further, beyond the U.S., there is extensive criminality south of the border and into South America, which stems from the drug funded cartels which supply the U.S.'s demand for drugs, and a large undocumented immigrant population who are fleeing from their lawless homelands. The exercise of the proxy vote will bring a bright spotlight to the entire drugs issue. Since parents are the most highly sensitized to these issues, the topic will naturally become much more central to public discourse. One or both of the political parties will seize the opportunity to develop and propose a serious plan, and some leader will become more willing to boldly step forward to begin the difficult process of beginning the national dialogue or argument. The specific changes are beyond the scope of this document, but given the number of lives lost, the effort is worthy of consideration, especially compared to the many issues which are discussed with great passion in the current political environment, but which affect very few citizens.

4) Increasing youth dissatisfaction with Capitalism and interest in Socialism

Recent surveys of the millennial generation indicate that this generation, roughly defined as currently between ages 17-37 years old is viewing socialism in a positive light.[59] According to a report from the Victims of Communism Memorial Foundation, based on YouGov survey results, 44 percent of millennials stated that they would rather live in a socialist than a capitalist society. Similar results were reported by the University of Chicago's GenForward Survey of Americans aged 18 to 34 which found that 45 percent have a favorable view of socialism, against 49 percent having a favorable view of capitalism (the term the press tends to use for free market economics). Some of this may be due to a lack of knowledge, somewhat suggested by a CBS/New York Times survey indicating that only 16 percent of millennials could accurately define socialism.[60] (Payton, 2017) They may envision something that is actually a rosy version of a social welfare democratic state in the model of Germany or a subset of Scandinavian nations without an understanding of the strictures and barriers that these states impose. They also would not likely know or understand that there is a trend in these states away from increasing taxation as the realities of the negative impact on their economies becomes more apparent and better understood.

This is a purely speculative viewpoint, but worth considering. There is good reason to believe that this rejection of free market economics or capitalism is a reflection of the millennials perception, largely accurate, of the bad deal that they and their families have been given under the current democratic system. That bad deal is not due to democracy or due to living in a free market economy, but rather due to their lack of representation. The discussion topics that we have covered in this chapter are not lost on them, though they do not recognize that the core of the problem is this lack of representation. The unfair situation that their families have experienced and that they see ahead is not due to the political idea of democracy, or the economic framework of a free market, but simply due to the gap in achieving an authentic democratic system. For the 20+ years of their lives, the current system has provided no representation of their needs and is therefore neglecting the issues and needs of their generation. Some of the shift of the balance of power has coincided with the rise of the power of all organizations, which affects all Americans, but the highest impact is on families that lack full representation, because of a shift towards a demographic with priorities quite distant from their needs.

It is this gap, and not evidence of a better model that is creating the interest in a different economic model. Young Americans are not concluding that the better option is what is currently occurring in

Venezuela, the tragedy of Cuba's long trek into deprivation and decline, the revolution in the former USSR and the chaos and horror which followed, or the repression within the People's Republic of China. All of the modern examples of communism and socialism have led to disaster. Perhaps there are a few idealistic zealots or the gullible and dutiful students of leftist-fascist professors who believe these offer a better way, but not the well informed. Those same students would refute the idea of socialism when presented with something less theoretical and closer to their life experience. For example, about how one is compensated for work or for their own academic performance; very few would agree that everyone should receive the same pay or grades, regardless of contribution or performance or results. Rather, the opinion reflects a recognition that the current U.S. system is not sufficiently fair to the young in its approach to balancing the needs and desires of its citizens. They may simply be concluding that the system is currently failing to meet its ideal of "all men are created equal" and properly supporting "life, liberty, and pursuit of happiness". With no apparent alternative, socialism may seem appealing – from the safe distance of a lack of experience with living in a socialist state.

CHAPTER 3

Movements Toward Authentic Democracy

———

BOTH DEFINITIONS OF DEMOCRACY IN Webster's Online Dictionary are adequately broad to allow many governments and institutions to claim to be democracies:

1) Government by the people; especially: rule of the majority; and
2) A government in which the supreme power is vested in the people and exercised by them directly or indirectly through a system of representation usually involving periodically held free elections.

The definition of "the people" can be restricted to a substantially small subset of the people or apply simply to the system of voting. The earliest democratic governments began with this limitation, limiting the democracy to the group which held economic and social and therefore political power. In the United States, the original declaration of "We the People" was made with a similarly limited perspective. The correction of these limits, i.e. the expansion of voting rights to most of the population, has been slow and often required a cataclysmic event as the final catalyst to force a change. The largest among these were the Civil War, World War I, and the Civil Rights Movement, each creating turmoil throughout the nation. Despite the simplicity of the concept of each citizen having a vote, this remains an area of contention and conflict today.

This brief summary cannot do justice to the history of democracy and would more accurately be described as a selection of events relevant to our current democracy. It is intended to highlight the major transformational changes in U.S. democracy, as a reminder for those with some knowledge and as a primer for those who were never introduced to the information in this context. The inclusion here is intended to highlight that the expansion of the vote to include all citizens towards authentic democracy is the natural evolutionary course towards full authentic democracy. The steps to achieve this were more revolutionary, than evolutionary, though the overall change has come as incremental steps towards the proper end goal of a vote for each citizen. At every step, there was stubborn resistance to the need for correction. Each time, the slowness in recognizing the need for change created discord and the resistance to change led to terrible consequences for the nation and for individual citizens.

This is also intended as an important reminder that our democracy was not crafted as a complete end product at its founding during the American Revolution. The vast expansion of the democracy was forged by those who came later - the abolitionists, the civil rights leaders, and the suffragists, many making grave personal sacrifices for what they deeply believed was the most important ideal of the American Revolution - legal and political equality for all citizens. The history of the nation's progress to date passes through great personal sacrifice and very real physical pain – not simply philosophical or intellectual debate - all to expand the power for self-determination to the full population. The same factors that have caused the continued development of our democracy were the same factors which were the initial seeds of the U.S. revolution - lack of fair representation for British Citizens of the colonies within the English Parliament.

We must learn to not take too long before the taking action on the next step in the evolution of our democracy. Historically, these steps have taken far too long and required great turmoil, personal suffering and sacrifice until the groups in control were willing to allow change. At nearly 100 years since women achieved suffrage in the United States, this democracy is still developing. Though we will not be faced with toddlers or families leading violent protests in the streets, we may find that there is intergenerational conflict and many other secondary effects which lead to civil disruption and decay. Or we may simply and unexpectedly create a dystopian civilization with population and quality of life decline for many years. Change is coming and we must decide how to adjust.

EARLY HISTORY OF DEMOCRACY

The term democracy derives from combining the Greek "demos" meaning common people and "kratos" rule or power. Athenian democracy is often used as the example of an early democratic government and is the source of the term. However, Athenian democracy was limited in a similar way to an oligarchy. As with an oligarchy, the power was shared by a subset of the population. However, that limited voting group was a much larger segment of the population and used democratic processes to make decisions. Athenian democracy was limited to the subset of the population who were adult males and was also bounded within age group and citizenship status. The number "varied between 30,000 and 50,000 out of a total population of around 250,000 to 300,000" or "no more than 30 percent of the total adult population",[61] (Thorley, 1996) a larger number than most oligarchies, but still far fewer than the full population. Over the 200 years or so of Athenian democracy, the system was not static and was often challenged and modified. The power was challenged by the aristocracy, replaced by a popular tyrant, modified to include additional groups of citizens, e.g. with expansion of voting to include new groups, like the citizens of Plataea and of Samos, and modified to change the balance between legislative powers and the courts.

The democracy of the Athenians was criticized even then as impractical and more recently in the 500 years before the American Revolution was viewed as a theoretical construct which was not workable, except within a total structure of a government combining monarchy with aristocracy, with elements of a constitutional democracy. The U.S. was modeled closer to Roman than to Greek democracy. "The classical example that inspired the American and French revolutionaries as well as the English radicals was Rome rather than Greece. Thus, the Founding Fathers who met in Philadelphia in 1787, did not set up a Council of Areopagos like the Greeks, but a Senate, that eventually met on a Capitol."[62] (Hanson, 2005)

HISTORY OF DEMOCRACY IN THE UNITED STATES: COLONIES TO INDEPENDENCE TO CIVIL WAR

The American Colonies declaring independence from Britain had similar governmental and legal systems, all modeled upon the British system. Each Colony was self-governing with some variation in structure and processes between them, and each holding their own local elections. The demand for independence derived directly from the colonists asserting their perceived right to determine the laws and taxes imposed by the government and to decide these through a representative government. The well-known slogan used before the Declaration of Independence, "No taxation without representation", was primarily in response to the many acts passed by the British Parliament which had a large effect upon the colonies, including the Navigation Acts (1651, 1663), followed by 3 additional in the 1760's - the Stamp Act (1764), Sugar Act (1765) and Quartering Act (1765). These had followed several other earlier acts of Parliament including the Hat Act (1732), Molasses Act (1733), and Iron Act (1750); all restricting trade by the American colonies to benefit Britain's economy. The colonists viewed these acts as imposed without their representation

in Parliament and without colonial government approval, therefore denying what colonists viewed as "their rights as Englishmen".[63]
(Blackstone, 1753) Those rights were specified under the British legal
system and detailed in Britain's Bill of Rights in 1689. It's not surprising that the King and Parliament did not view the issues in the same
way. At that time "the British Parliament was quite unrepresentative.
The British Parliament largely was based on men who were elected
from the small towns and farmlands and not from the burgeoning
big cities that were growing up with the Industrial Revolution. So
Manchester or Birmingham didn't have any seats in Parliament, and
the British said, `Why are you complaining, you in America? The same
thing's true over here. We're not representative, but we're happy.'"[64]
(Weintraub, 2005)

While the colonists were protesting this lack of representation in
Parliament, the colonists' governments were themselves also not representative, since they excluded many different categories of citizens
from both political and civil rights within every colony. Since the colonies legal and governance practices derived directly from European
practices, this was simply consistent with the models of European government of the time. The conventional criteria for the vote were male,
white, and landowning, and these same criteria continued for some
time. There were additional barriers, based on religion before the
Revolution, which was common to Europe, with its long and difficult
history of religious conflict.

Most European nations had long denied political and many civil
rights to alien religious denominations following the Reformation.
In Britain, the Test Acts of 1672 and 1678, prevented Non-Anglicans,
meaning Roman Catholics and non-Anglican Protestants, from holding public office by requiring a declaration or oath of office that was in
conflict with those religions The Disenfranchising Act of 1727, was one
of the later Penal Laws which prohibited all Roman Catholics from voting and remained in effect until 1793. Roman Catholics continued to
be prevented from running for office in the House of Commons until

1829 with the 1829 Catholic Relief Act. Non-Anglican Protestants were permitted to run beginning 1828.

After the signing of the Declaration of Independence several colonies continued to maintain religious barriers, denying voting rights, along with prohibiting the holding of government offices for Catholics, Quakers and Jews. In Georgia, the 1777 Constitution indicated that representatives "shall be of the Protestant religion". The 1778 Constitution of the State of South Carolina similarly limited the leading roles in government to Protestants and limited those who would vote upon those roles to be Protestants.[65] (Carolina, 1778) In Maryland, voting rights and eligibility were withheld from Jewish Americans and these restrictions continued until 1828.[66]

The United States Constitution left each state with the power to define voting eligibility at ratification in 1789. Voting eligibility differed by state but was generally limited to property-owning or tax-paying white males, yielding only 6% of the population eligible at ratification. The property ownership requirement changed in each state over a long period, and was finally eliminated in all states by 1856, with four states retaining the tax-paying requirements until 1860, and two until the 20th century. The Constitution also distributed members of the House of Representatives proportionally per state by population, which included the slave population - oddly counted as 3/5 per person; that did not mean providing a vote or representation for that group, but rather weighting the distribution of House members to include that calculation, providing legislative advantages to white voters in southern states during the early years of the republic.

The expansion of voting rights since ratification of the U.S. Constitution has been slow and sporadic. The first federal change came soon after ratification with the Naturalization Act of 1790, establishing the requirements for foreign born residents of the U.S. to become citizens: "...any alien, being a free white person, who having resided within the limits and jurisdiction of the United States for a term of two years........of good character" is eligible to apply for citizenship. The act also states that children who are born abroad to parents who are U.S. citizens are considered citizens.

ABOLITION MOVEMENT TO THE 15TH AMENDMENT

The landmark changes to the Constitution, those affecting the largest populations and still best remembered, came after the Civil War: the 15th Amendment (1870) "not be denied.....by any State on account of race, color, or previous condition of servitude; 19th Amendment (1920): "....not be denied ....by any State on account of sex."; and 24th Amendment (1964): " not be denied ...... by the United States or any State by reason of failure to pay any poll tax or other tax." In each case, demands for change began many years before there was a constitutional change, and in each case there was tremendous civil and political conflict before there was sufficient popular support among the voting popula- tion and sufficient energy and foresight within Congress to lead a change for a potential constituency that didn't initially have political power.

The path to the vote and more broadly to full suffrage for minori- ties and women had its roots in the abolition movement. In the late 17th and early 18th century small groups began calling for an end to the slave trade and to free those in slavery in Europe and in the North American colonies. The Mennonites, Quakers and early Evangelical Christian groups were the most prominent, condemning slavery as con- trary to Christian tenets. The message of spiritual equality was a core message of the Protestant revivalist movement of the 1730s and 1740s known as the First Great Awakening, which required the abolition of slavery.

In the two decades following the Revolution, each of the Northern states individually passed legislation abolishing slavery. In some cases, the actual emancipation was gradual, for example not freeing the slaves themselves but allowing their children to be born free. In 1807 the U.S. passed the Act Prohibiting Importation of Slaves as federal law, doing just what the name of the Act states, banning the importation of slaves into the United States. (Article 1 Section 9 of the Constitution had protected the slave trade from being banned for 20 years, not permitting a change until 1808, which is when this act took effect.) This did not eliminate the slave trade within the United States; slavery and trade in slaves remained legal, but it reduced the importation by over 90%. Slaves continued to be imported illegally, with up to 50,000 smuggled through Texas and Florida before these states were admitted into the Union.[67] (Sparks)

The economic systems, values, and political viewpoints between states in the North and South were quite different and continued to diverge into the early 19th century. By 1820, the legislation commonly known as the Missouri Compromise was the temporary resolution to an early political conflict between the northern and southern states over whether Missouri would be admitted as a slave holding state, potentially shifting the balance of power between slave owning and Free states. The compromise gave statehood to Missouri with a state constitution permitting legal slavery, but at the same time outlawing the legality of slavery in the remaining territory of the Louisiana Purchase - the area which was not yet organized into specific new territories. This is the area which later became Arkansas and Oklahoma.

The Missouri Compromise also included the entry of the free state of Maine to statehood. The Missouri Compromise was later declared unconstitutional as a part of the appalling Dred Scott Supreme Court landmark decision of 1857. The court found that "a Negro, whose ancestors were imported into [the U.S.], and sold as slaves", could not be a citizen so that freedom gave no standing as a citizen to sue in federal court. In addition to the Dred Scott's case finding of the Missouri Compromise to be unconstitutional, it also found that slaves were private property and that Congress did not have the power to regulate slavery in the territories, and could not revoke a slave owner's rights based on where he lived. The political fallout of Dred Scott led to increased conflict and served as an important catalyst to the Civil War.

Roots of Abolition in Europe

Western European nations with colonies had long struggled with the ethical and moral inconsistences between their national movements towards representative governments for their own citizens, consistent with their religious beliefs requiring equality, compassion, and justice on the one side, with the severe cruelty and oppression that was central to slavery on the other. By 1807, Britain banned the importation of African slaves to its colonies. By 1833, Britain further abolished slavery across the British Empire in the Slavery Abolition Act of 1833, with the important and enormous exceptions of "any Territories in the Possession of the East India Company, or to the Island of Ceylon, or to the Island of Saint Helena." These exceptions were removed ten years later in 1843. To smooth the transition for slaveholders, The Abolition Act of 1833 included compensation for slaveholders paid for by the government. This compensation over the following years was in the range of 5% of GDP in compensation to slaveholders for freed slaves, a significant outlay representing roughly 40% of the then normal year of total government expenditure. The end of slavery was not immediate, first converting slaves into "apprentices", finally ending in 1840. Slavery was later finally abolished in India by the Indian Slavery Act of 1843.

France was much earlier in recognizing the profound evil of slavery and took steps towards abolition much earlier. In 1315, Louis X decreed that any slave setting foot within the Kingdom of France would be freed. In 1685, King Louis XIV's Code Noir decree provided a legal framework for slavery in the colonies, beginning to offer some modest legal rights to the slave (e.g. Masters who killed their slaves would be punished), and established rules surrounding religious practice, and rules around the activities of free people of African descent. It was slowly implemented in the colonies including in the West Indies in 1687, Guyana in 1704, Reunion in 1723, and Louisiana in 1724. It was not intended for, nor applied to the Canadian French colony which had few slaves.

In 1794, as a result of the French Revolution, France's First Republic abolished slavery in France and its colonies, granting full citizenship to former slaves, and paying compensation from the government to the former slaveholders. By 1802 it was reestablished under Napoleon to maintain political control over the colonies. It was not until 1848 that the Second Republic of France abolished slavery in its colonies.

Spain's history of slavery was very different, with an extensive history of slavery dating back to the Romans. During the years of Muslim Spain, or Al-Andalus from the early 8th century to late in the 15th century, the Muslim Moors imported white Christian slaves from the Christian section of Spain and later from the Orthodox Christian areas of the Mediterranean. The Iberian Peninsula served as a base for further export of Christians to Muslim nations and North Africa. After the fall of the last Muslim state on the Iberian Peninsula in 1492 to the Christian kingdoms of the north, the religions placed under slavery reversed, with the captured Moors and captives from North Africa often forced into bondage. By the 16th century, Spain had the highest proportion of African slaves among European nations. In 1542, Charles V, Emperor of the Holy Roman Empire, issued a decree (Leyes Nuevas or New Laws) abolishing the enslavement of natives. However, the forced labor of native peoples continued illegally into the next century, along with legal black slave labor and participation in the slave trade. Prior to 1800, Spain was far less involved in the African slave trade than the other leading colonial nations, responsible for 61,000 slaves of the 7 million embarking on ships during those years.[68] (Emory)

However, during the next century Spain increased its involvement in the slave trade, just as Britain and France were reducing and then discontinuing their involvement. In the 19th century, Spain increased its trade to over 470K slaves embarking on ships, sending most to the Caribbean and Cuba. This was second only to Portugal in that century, which moved over 2.4 million in the 19th century, primarily to Brazil. For comparison, this is over 8 times the number embarked to the U.S. during 3 centuries of slavery. (Emory)

Slavery has not been limited to the Europeans, and spans across many cultures, continents, nations, and religions, with most imperial nations having a history of some form of slavery. Indigenous cultures are also not exempt, stretching back to earliest human societies. In the Ottoman Empire it was a significant element of the society and the empire's economy, with up to 20% of the population in slavery in the city of Constantinople, the political center of the Empire, by the early 17th century. Under the devsime or "blood tax", young Christian boys from Anatolia and the Balkans were taken from their families converted to Islam and enlisted in the military Janissaries, a soldier class. Customs statistics indicate that Constantinople's importation of slaves during the 16th and 17th century from the Black Sea reached 2.5 million people. By the early 19th century under pressure from Europeans, several legal acts were passed limiting enslavement of people with white skin, and by 1830, the Sultan issued a decree which gave freedom to white slaves. Slavery continued in the Ottoman Empire until the Empire was defeated and partitioned by the Allied Powers after World War I.

The 20th century continued the progress towards illegalizing slavery worldwide with the UN's 1948 adoption of Universal Declaration of Human Rights – Article 4, and in 2004 the Arab League's Arab Charter on Human Rights. Despite the progress, slavery continues today.[69] (PolarisProject.Org) The International Labour Organization, an agency of the UN estimates that "20.9 million women, men and children are trapped in jobs into which they were coerced or deceived and which they cannot leave" as of 2017.[70] (Organization, 2019)

The European and United States abolition movements overlapped in time and grew from similar religious and moral roots. Over the first half of the 19th century, the abolitionists were quite successful in outlawing slavery within Great Britain and in the northern states of the US. In 1807, Jefferson signed the Act Prohibiting the Importation of Slaves which was implemented in 1808, the soonest that it could be implemented due to a restriction in Section 9 of the Constitution.

In the South, slavery was legally well embedded. The abolitionist movements emerged nearly entirely in the north and were perceived by southern states as interfering in their legal systems, encouraging fugitive or 'runaway' slaves and inciting rebellion. The concern was a large part of the motivation for the Fugitive Slave Act of 1850, which required the northern states to return fugitive slaves and established legal ground for draconian measures to enforce the return of slaves across state lines. Special commissioners were established with jurisdiction alongside the normal U.S. circuit and district courts and the courts of territories to enforce the law. The law provided Commissioners with a financial incentive for making decisions favoring slaveholders, for example, doubling the fee that commissioners received in cases where the findings concluded in favor of the slaveholders, (the window dressing on this was that it was for the extra paperwork required of commissioners to arrange transport back to the owner.) Penalties were placed upon anyone who aided slaves to escape and upon marshals who refused to enforce the law. It additionally allowed marshals to force private citizens into service in a posse. Those accused as fugitive slaves could not testify in court and no trial by jury was permitted.

The severity of this act led to gross abuse and intensified the resistance to enforcing Slave laws by citizens in northern states. It also greatly heightened concerns about the many warping effects of allowing slavery to continue within the US. Many thought that the actions of commissioners and the required delivery of slaves violated state sovereignty and states' rights. Between 1850 and 1858, new personal liberty laws were enacted in eight northern states to provide some civil rights to accused slaves. In 1854, Wisconsin's Supreme Court declared the Fugitive Slave Law unconstitutional. The most lasting political outcome of the Fugitive Slave Act was to substantially heighten northern attention to southern slavery and to increase the number of abolitionists.

From 1815 through the early 1850's numerous abolitionist organizations, at least 15 core organizations, were formed throughout the northern states. The largest and most influential abolition organization was the American Anti-Slavery Society (AASS) which grew to 250 thousand members across 2,000 affiliated groups. The AAS was founded by William Lloyd Garrison in 1833, demanding the immediate abolition of slavery in the US, after earlier co-founding the weekly anti-slavery newspaper, *The Liberator*. The potential threat posed by anti-slavery organizations and their activity drew violent reaction from slave interests in both the Southern and Northern states. Mobs attacked anti-slavery meetings, assaulted lecturers, ransacked offices, burned postal sacks of pamphlets, and destroyed the organization's presses. Garrison was the target of Southern state bounties for his capture, "dead or alive".[71] In one incident, when Garrison was scheduled to address a meeting in Boston, he was taken by a mob and pulled through the streets, intending to 'tar and feather' him; only the mayor's intervention to arrest him for his safety saved his life.

Beyond abolition, Garrison was also a firm advocate for women's rights. His commitment to woman's rights and to their full participation in the abolition movement led some male group members to leave to form another organization in 1840, with others leaving because of his commitment that the group not participate in the government or in politics. His reasoning was primarily centered on the conclusion that the Constitution was pro-slavery, since it explicitly outlined rules to protect slavery. At the international World Anti-Slavery Convention in London, in 1840, when the convention refused to seat the American women delegates, Garrison and the other male delegates of the American group joined the women in the spectator's gallery. The controversy was another introduction of woman's rights issues to England. It was also an early introduction to the issue of woman's rights for Elizabeth Cady Stanton, who attended the convention as a spectator accompanying her husband, Henry B. Stanton, who was a delegate.

By the end of 1840, Garrison announced the formation of another organization, the Friends of Universal Reform, with sponsors and founding members including prominent reformers Maria Chapman,

Abby Kelley Foster, Oliver Johnson, and Amos Bronson Alcott (father of Louisa May Alcott). The abolitionists across all of the organizations influenced the movement within the north to abolish slavery, but they did not greatly influence the legislation that finally eliminated slavery nationally, nor did they ever reach the level of ensuring suffrage. Much of the abolitionists' progress was still blocked by the realities of the south's economy. The abolition movement may have laid the ground-work towards abolition, but the seminal event, the Emancipation Proclamation, was driven by the Civil War and empowered by Lincoln's War Powers due to the southern state's succession.

The pre-Civil War southern states were much more rural and agrarian than the north. The central economic engine of their agrarian economy was the large plantation growing cash crops served by the surrounding small towns, and many small farms. The urban north in contrast relied on industry and commerce within larger urban areas as the central economic engine. In 1860, southern cities and state capitals were small and few, and none were industrial. Of the top 25 cities of the U.S., only 3 were in the south, New Orleans, Charleston and Richmond, with populations of 160,000, 40,000 and 38,000, ranking 6th, 22nd and 25th. The three together were about one sixth the size of the top 3 northern cities, and less than 10% the size of the top 10 northern cities.

The economic differences between the northern and southern states and the personal economics of their citizens was a major con-tributing factor to the inevitable conflict. By the 1860 U.S. census, the slave population had grown to 4 million people, with 2.3 million slaves in the first 7 states to secede, another 1.2 million in 4 states that joined the separation, with 550,000 in slave states which did not secede. In the southern states, slaves made up 38% of the population and were centrally important to the economics of the plantation. Approximately 31% of households owned slaves at the outbreak of the civil war with most slaves on the larger plantations.[72] (Ransom) By 1860, slavery was responsible for 31 percent of the earnings in the state for the first 7 seceding states.[73] (Gunderson, 1974) Since the Northern States traded heavily with the south, many northerners also believed that abolition would be economically devastating to the nation, consequently many in the North also supported the status quo and opposed the abolitionists, based on economics, not morality.

	Slave population percent of total Population	Per Capita Earnings of Free Population (dollars)	Value of Slave Earnings Per Free Population (dollars)	Fraction of Earnings Due to Slavery
Alabama	45	120	50	41.7
South Carolina	57	159	57	35.8
Florida	44	143	48	33.6
Georgia	44	136	40	29.4
Mississippi	55	253	74	29.2
Louisiana	47	229	54	23.6
Texas	30	134	26	19.4
Seven Cotton States Average	46	163	50	30.6

Fraction of State Income from Slavery State Percent of the Population in 1860 (Gunderson, 1974)

The earlier actions to end slavery in France in 1794, and Britain in 1833, included compensation from the government to slaveholders to compensate for the loss of asset value. In the U.S., it seems that no similar proposal gained ground and is not part of the historical record. The size and value of the slave population may have simply been too large for Congress to consider compensation, with the cost of the "stock of slaves" approaching $2.7 Billion in 1860 dollars, compared to U.S. Federal spending that year of $180M.[74] (Goldin, 1973 (34)) It would have required doubling the nation's budget for 15 years to pay off, without considering interest. Tragically, the actual costs of the Civil War were much higher than the suggested asset value of the 'stock of slaves', including $3.3 Billion in government expense, $1.5 Billion in physical destruction, and extensive indirect costs estimated at close at $10

Billion when longer term effects are included.[75] Incomparably more important were the 625 – 750,000 battle deaths, and up to another 250,000 other deaths including 60,000 civilians and well over 60,000 slave deaths which were counted, and many others which remained undocumented.[76] Beyond deaths were casualties, other horrors and shattered lives. The deaths totaled roughly 4.3% of the U.S. population, proportionally the equivalent of 14 million of the current U.S. population. As high as these losses were, the huge numbers understate the direct personal impact for citizens in the southern states. During the four years of war, over 1 million soldiers are estimated to have served in the Confederate military at some time, or roughly 38% of the white male population of 5.5 Million. Confederate military deaths, were estimated at approximately 290,000 or 10.5% of the white male population or nearly 30% of white males between ages 18 and 45.[77]

Lincoln cannot be considered to be an abolitionist in the sense of the term defined as someone demanding the immediate end to slavery. However, he clearly considered slavery to be immoral, and was an opponent of the systems which supported it. In the Lincoln-Douglas Senate debate of 1858, Lincoln warned of the power of the plantation owners and the danger to republicanism, then known as 'Slave Power', though Lincoln did not use that term. Upon Lincoln's election as President, Lincoln's Republican Party platform was not abolitionist, but rather designed to achieve the gradual elimination of slavery. In fact, Lincoln quietly supported the Corwin Amendment, which had passed Congress before his election, written to guarantee to the southern states that the increase in 'free' states would not be used to interfere with slavery in the slave states without Southern consent. This was one of many measures offered to attempt to convince the southern states to remain in the Union. After Congressional approval, the Corwin Amendment was never ratified by the states as events overtook the practicality of that offered concession.

Between Lincoln's Presidential victory and his inauguration 3 months later, the 7 'Deep South' cotton states seceded, forming the Confederate States. Civil War began when Confederate soldiers fired upon Union troops at Fort Sumter, South Carolina in April 1861. When Lincoln called for troops from each state to suppress the rebellion, four additional southern slave states joined the Confederates.

After nearly 2 years of war with the Confederate states, Lincoln issued the Emancipation Proclamation in January of 1863, which changed the legal status of the 3 million slaves in the Confederacy from slave to free. This did not free slaves in states that did not secede from the Union, since Lincoln's legal powers were limited to war powers over the seceding states. Though legally free, it would take some time before that legal freedom became a reality. Only former slaves behind Union lines and those able to escape were freed, until the Union lines finally moved forward to cover all Confederate territory on June 19, 1865. The 13th Amendment to the U.S. Constitution abolishing slavery through-out the United States was finally ratified and in full effect in December 1865, abolishing slavery in the U.S. and among the Indian tribes. In 1868, the 14th Amendment was ratified and in 1870 the 15th, grant-ing equal protection and citizenship rights and prohibiting states and the federal government from denying the right to vote based on "race, color, or previous condition of servitude".

In the years which followed, new barriers to the vote continued to be raised. Many states found ways to create new limitations through poll taxes, literacy tests, whites-only primaries, grandfather clauses and violent intimidation, all intended to systematically suppress African-American votes. These remained a fundamental component of the political process in several states for the next 95 years. In 1882, the Chinese Exclusion Act barred immigrants of Chinese ethnicity from becoming U.S. citizens. In 1876, the Supreme Court found that Native Americans were explicitly excluded from the Fourteenth Amendment and therefore not granted citizenship rights. In 1887, the Dawes Act granted some Native Americans voting rights under very specific condi-tions. The Dawes Act, was designed to break up tribes as a social unit and redistribute land to white settlers, with the aspirational intention of lifting the Native Americans out of poverty and fostering assimilation into mainstream American society. It was clearly not intended to shift political power to Native Americans through the vote. In 1890, Congress passed the Indian Naturalization Act which permitted Native Americans in Indian Territory to apply for citizenship status in federal courts, and in 1924 Congress passes the Indian Citizenship Act, granting full citizenship rights (which were not accepted by all tribal nations).

THE WOMEN'S RIGHTS MOVEMENT TO THE 19TH AMENDMENT

A comprehensive history of the movement for Women's Suffrage in the United States is beyond the scope of this document. However, since it is an example of the progress towards Authentic Democracy, it is worth scanning the history here. Moreover, since the education of many Americans, including mine, focused nearly exclusively on the women's suffrage movement in the early 20th century, and was relatively thin on that, it is worth this slightly broader introduction. It's hard to believe that the movement doubled the number of voting citizens and is still covered as a secondary event instead of a principal movement in the development of the American Democracy and in the progress towards providing true legal and social justice. There is much to learn from this critical movement and its implication for Authentic Democracy through the proxy vote. If reading this brief primer leads some to want to learn more about the Women's Suffrage movement and pick up a book by a history scholar, then it has served a good purpose.

"The very truths you are now contending for, will,
in fifty years, be so embedded in public opinion
that no one need say one word in their defense"

—ANGELINA GRIMKE WELD
(To Elizabeth Cady Stanton)

The women's suffrage movement in the United States was long, slow, and circuitous, with many promising paths and initiatives showing progress, but most never directly leading to any additional rights, nor the vote. The movement spanned a lifetime between the early advocacy and conventions to final ratification of the 19th amendment in 1920; that is 72 years after the first organized convention in 1848, the Seneca Falls Convention for women's rights; and 50 years after the ratification of the 15th amendment prohibiting denial of the right to vote based on race in 1870, and 42 years after the introduction to Congress of the Women's Suffrage Amendment in 1878. Angelina Grimke's prediction *(above)* that public opinion would eventually align with beliefs championed by the movement was exactly correct, but it was closer to 100 years rather than 50 for full acceptance, spanning several generations of Americans before there was full acceptance of the democratic and legal rights of women.

After the ratification of the U.S. Constitution, women were not permitted to vote, except for very unique exceptions. (The most notable exceptions were in NJ, ended by a law in 1807, and in Kentucky for a small group of widows who paid taxes.) Perhaps the earliest written philosophical articulation of the demand for women's rights that influenced western culture was written in 1791 by Olympe de Gouges in *Declaration of the Rights of Woman and the Female Citizen*, during the period of turmoil immediately following the French Revolution. Gouges was already known as a human rights activist and playwright, most notably for a 1785 play *l'Esclavage des Noirs"*, (translated Black Slavery), which was actively sabotaged by the slave trade lobby through a press campaign and audience hecklers. The Declaration was written in response to the *Declaration of the Rights of Man and of the Citizen*, the newly adopted human civil rights document written by Lafayette, in consultation with Thomas Jefferson, and adopted by the revolutionary period National Constituent Assembly in 1789. The Rights of Woman mirrored The Rights of Man, highlighting the failures in the promise of the French Revolution towards promoting equality for women. As a result of this and other publications, Gouges was convicted of treason and beheaded in 1793 during the mass executions of the Girondins, a loosely affiliated group of moderates of the National Assembly.

Three years after the publication of The Rights of Woman, Mary Wollstonecraft published the essay "A Vindication of the Rights of a Woman: with Strictures on Political and Moral Subjects in England." This was a response to another of the many documents related to human rights written early in the French Revolutionary period: Talleyrand's report to the French National Assembly recommending a national system of public education. The report recommended that only men should receive public education and that women should be educated in the home, ".....more suited to a calm and secluded life." By today's standards, Wollstonecraft's essay cannot be considered to be an argument for women's rights but is instead simply an argument for some improvement to the dynamic of that time and is much milder than Olympe de Gouges' clear call for equal rights. It only argues that women should receive an education, and for moral equality between the sexes, but never suggests equality. It doesn't discuss full legal rights, nor the broader group of citizen's rights, nor the vote.

In the United States, it was not the vote, but the broader range of women's legal and societal rights that led to the first philosophical writings advocating for women's rights. The energy and principles which led several women to begin to call for expanding women's rights emerged from the organized abolition movement. When Sarah and Angelina Grimke began to write and speak out publicly on abolition, they became the targets of personal attacks and criticism, challenging the right of women to participate in public affairs and the propriety of public speeches to audiences of men and women. In 1837, Sarah published a series of letters in a Massachusetts newspaper, "Letters on the Equality of the Sexes and the Condition of Women", making a largely biblical and logical argument for women's rights. In 1843, Margaret Fuller published "The Great Lawsuit. Man versus Men. Woman versus

Women", making a scholarly argument that intellectual and spiritual freedom for women will benefit all mankind.

The first women's rights convention, the 1848 Seneca Falls (NY) Convention, was organized by local area female Quakers, along with Elisabeth Cady Stanton, already well known as an abolitionist, and timed to coincide with the visit of Lucretia Mott, an abolitionist and well known speaker and Quaker. The two-day convention covered several topics and reviewed a prepared Declaration of Sentiments, which included direct language calling for women's right to vote and all rights and privileges of a citizen of the United States. After heated debate on whether to include the demand of a woman's right to vote, Fredrick Douglas, already known as an abolitionist, speaker, and author, urged inclusion of the call for the right to vote. The Declaration was included and signed by 100 of the approximately 300 attendees. Over the next ten years, 1850-1860, National Women's Rights Conventions were held nearly annually. These were discontinued during the Civil War as the focus of women's activism shifted to emancipation and the end of slavery. In 1864, the Woman's National Loyal League, exercised unprecedented national political power by gathering 400,000 signatures, the largest petition drive to that time, petitioning Congress to pass the thirteenth amendment, abolishing slavery.

At the first women's rights convention after the conclusion of the Civil War in 1866, the convention attendees voted to create the American Equal Rights Association, to campaign for equal rights and suffrage for all citizens. While initially a unified group, all sharing the same core objectives of universal suffrage, by 1869 the group split into two factions, one more willing to postpone pushing for immediate women's suffrage to allow suffrage for African-American males to proceed with less political resistance; the second group believed that allowing African-American male enfranchisement without including women would only further exacerbate the difference in equality between the sexes. The first group was the National Women's Suffrage

Organization, (NWSA), with Lucy Stone, Julia Ward Howe and Henry Blackwell, among others.

The second group, the American Woman's Suffrage Association (AWSA), included Susan B. Anthony and Elizabeth Cady Stanton (Stanton and Matilda Joselyn Gage later wrote *History of Woman's Suffrage*, between 1876 and 1920, which captures the long struggle for suffrage, so naturally a good deal of the best documented history of the suffrage movement emphasized their activities above those of the first group.) The second group argued that the newly enfranchised black men will be more opposed to women's suffrage and that allowing their vote without women's suffrage would further delay women's suffrage. As debate began on the 15th amendment prohibiting the denial of voting rights based on race, both groups initially advocated for the inclusion of women's suffrage. The first group, including Lucy Stone finally decide that they should support the 15th amendment, hoping that alignment with the Republican Party's push for the amendment would help lead to their later support of universal suffrage. Frederick Douglass, long a supporter of women's rights sided with the first group stating that the franchise was a matter of life and death for former slaves.

The second group continued to actively oppose the amendment, believing that it would lead to inevitable extensive delay in women's suffrage (certainly the prediction of delay was accurate, at 50 additional years, but it's impossible to assess what would have happened if both groups continued to oppose the amendment.) Unfortunately, in the heat of the battle, Stanton's speeches during this time turned into what would today be termed racist rants, but it is ungenerous to not realize that she was limited by the understanding and education of that time, and frustrated by the resistance to the obvious need for equality from the group of leaders and male citizens holding the voting power. When the fifteenth amendment was passed in 1870, the primary political justification for the split in the suffrage groups was removed, but heated disagreement led the two groups to remain split before recombining 20 years later in 1890.

During that period of two groups, several different paths to gaining suffrage were tried. The first group, the NWSA, pursued the New Departure strategy, based on the idea that the Constitution implicitly enfranchised women. Beginning in 1871, hundreds of women tried to vote, leading to a lawsuit to try to enforce the votes being counted. Finally, the DC District Court found "The fact that the practical working of the assumed right would be destructive of civilization is decisive that the right does not exist."[78] (Elizabeth Cady Stanton, 1887) (Hard to believe that this logic and language could come from a court, but true.) In 1875, the Supreme Court finally ruled that the Constitution does not confer voting rights on anyone, and as a result, the NWSA redirected efforts towards promoting a voting rights amendment. In 1878, Senator Aaron Sargent introduced an amendment to Congress with text identical to the 15th amendment except that it prohibited denial because of sex, instead of 'denial due to race, color, or previous condition of servitude.' The amendment then sat in committee until it reached a vote in 1887, where it was rejected by 34-16.

By 1890, the two woman's suffrage organizations merged into one, the National American Woman Suffrage Association (NAWSA), and redirected efforts from winning at the national level, to winning public support, and winning at the state level. They needed to shift public opinion by convincing many women who did not care about the issue, win male voters, and convince state legislators that women's suffrage would benefit all of society. Between 1890 and 1896, some progress was made with 4 of the 46 states granting some level of women's suffrage: Colorado (1893), Utah and Idaho (1896), adding to Wyoming which was admitted to Union in 1890 already granting full voting rights for women. (In Wyoming, it was full suffrage and passed in the first session of the Territorial Legislature in 1869.) However, between 1896 and 1910, progress on states slowed and there were no new additional states[79] (Schons, 2011) granting voting rights.

In 1900, Carrie Chapman Catt became the President of NAWSA, as the chosen successor of Susan B. Anthony, who by then had been

President for 8 years and was 80 years of age. Ms. Catt had already brought renewed energy and focus to NAWSA when she earlier led the Organizational Committee, establishing state level goals and work plans for each state every year, and raising money to place a team of organizers into the field. As President, she outlined the strategic priorities for NAWSA, reestablishing focus on passing the federal amendment especially in states that already granted the right to vote in presidential elections, continuing efforts at the state level towards amending state constitutions, and implementing a southern strategy for gaining the right to vote in primaries in southern states. This established a strong foundation for the organization's future. In 1904 Catt resigned to care for her ailing husband, and was succeeded by Anna Howard Shaw, a physician and one of the first ordained female Methodist ministers. Howard continued in that role until 1915, when she resigned and was succeeded by Catt.

By 1910, NAWSA had grown to 117,000 members. Public opinion in the U.S. had begun to shift towards the movement along with a higher acceptance of movement member activities as a respectable endeavor for middle class women. Momentum for women's suffrage at the state level resumed in 1910 with Washington; California in 1911; Oregon, Arizona, Kansas in 1912; Illinois in 1913; Arkansas, Nebraska, New York (the first eastern state), North Dakota, in 1917; so that fourteen of the 48 states had some level of women's suffrage by 1917.

When the U.S. entered World War 1 in 1917, many NAWSA members were against U.S. involvement or politically active pacifists, but Ms. Catt made the controversial decision to lead NAWSA to actively support the war effort, launching groups within NAWSA for Food Conservation, Protection of Women in Industry, and Overseas Hospitals[80] (Turning Point Suffragist Memorial), and collaborating with other women's groups to support the war. By 1915, NAWSA was a formidable organization, with 44 state organizations, each with local chapters, totaling over 2 million members, and able to make a powerful and significant impact nationally. Women became involved in the war effort at the Homefront, working in munitions production and other defense work, in jobs usually handled by men, in supporting the government fund raising efforts through liberty loan drives, and in leading the food conservation program to conserve food needed by soldiers overseas.[81] (Hughes, 2017)

Beyond the movement, women also became actively involved in the overseas war effort. During the course of the war, 21,500 women served as nurses; 13,000 women served active duty in the Navy, 450 women served as switchboard operators supporting the western front in the Signal Corps Female Telephone Operators, which required bilingual English and French; along with other overseas contributions as ambulance drivers, in humanitarian relief, as linguists, etc. NAWSA's support for the war effort began to turn the tide of public opinion, while the state by state efforts continued. Michigan, Oklahoma, South Dakota in 1918; and Indiana in 1919, so that 16 of the then 48 states had some level of women's suffrage by 1919. As the momentum of public opinion shifted, and the number of state legislatures with women constituents increased, the energy at the federal level shifted in favor of ratification of the 19th amendment. Although Congress had a tacit agreement to not raise legislation that was not war related during the war years, the House passed the amendment 304 to 89 in 1918. In 1919, the Senate passed the amendment on the third try, 56 to 25. The legislature of Tennessee passed the amendment in August 1920 and it became the law of the land. The United Kingdom had granted women's suffrage two years earlier to the subset of women over 30, later amended in 1928 to all women over 21 under the same terms as men.

This excerpted history of the last few pages omitted many initiatives and major events that did not directly lead to ratification of the amendment and it is difficult to determine which are simply less visibly influential on the outcome, but essential as catalysts. Reviewing the history at that level is well beyond the objectives or capability of this scan and requires deep understanding of that time in U.S. history. The most important among the areas not covered: 1) The impact of the struggle for Suffrage in the United Kingdom, which prior to 1918 did not yet allow universal male suffrage, barring more than 70% of males from parliamentary elections. The British movement covered roughly the same period and intensified at the turn of the century and turned far more militant. One of the leading Suffrage groups, the Women's Social and Political Union (WSPU), led by Emmeline Pankhurst, sought to publicize the movement using activist means, which included both less violent means like rallies, parades, sit-ins and hunger strikes, and heckling members of parliament, along with more violent and destructive means like arson of unoccupied churches and country houses, assaulting police, stone-throwing, window-smashing, and shouting down speakers. During marches, mobs of spectators, and the police often responded with violent force, increasing the animus and turmoil. News reports of the UK movement activity certainly influenced U.S. citizens and the suffrage movement in the U.S., and the full history is worthy of study, but would require an extensive digression here.

The second area not covered is related to the first. The most direct impact in the U.S. of the U.K. movement was in the formation of the National Women's Party (NWP), founded in 1916 by Alice Paul and Lucy Burns, both having earlier involvement with the Pankhurst family and the WSPU. The NWP followed a similar activist strategy to the British WSPU, with positions very different from the NAWSA, for example taking a neutral stance on the war rather than supporting it, continuing militant activities after war was declared, actively opposing President Wilson's Democratic Party in elections, etc. Their pickets, strikes, hunger strikes and the violent mistreatment they received attracted news coverage and many believe this influenced the progress towards the Amendment. Some scholars argue that these were as influential as the NAWSA's influence to overcome the resistance to the 19th Amendment. For the purpose of this discussion on the movement towards authentic democracy, the efforts of the NWP are an important example of citizens seeking to find a different path to overcome the many obvious barriers that were in place over so many years, which prevented women from achieving suffrage in the U.S. Many women suffered life threatening violence, pain, deprivation and alienation, and took extreme personal risk to fight for equal rights and the vote.

The last important area is the aftermath of ratification. Poll taxes, literacy tests, residency requirements, along with social beliefs and familiarity continued to limit the number of women voting for some time, but by 1960, women were showing a higher level of participation in presidential elections than men. Until 1980, women did not demonstrate party alignment different from men, but since that time, some level of voting gender gap favoring the Democratic Party has repeated in presidential elections, ranging from a low of 6 percentage points higher in 1984 to a high of 11 points in 1996 and 2016.

The expansion of the vote to nearly all adult citizens, finally occurred with the 15th and 19th Amendments, but at a cost of many lives and required the sacrifice and dedication of the lifetimes of the many women and men who could perceive that there would be no justice until citizens had an equal voice. Many realized that the vote was only a step in the process of gaining equality and justice, and that time would be required to make societal change happen, but they believed it was an essential step and worth fighting for.

The women and men who fought for suffrage were on the right side of history, of course, and citizens of the 21st century see this as self-evident. The nation lost much because of the delay in the willingness of citizens with the vote to accept the change, and then for it to be fully enforced through the Voting Rights Act of 1965. Loss in lives, in lifetimes of conflict, loss in treasure, and in the effects upon every individual citizen who lived their lives in a society of injustice. The opportunity cost that was lost to the nation may be higher – meaning that the advancement of the nation across all important dimensions would have been so much faster if we had removed the constraints to education and work for women and minorities sooner. Simply listening and meeting the demands for equal citizenship in voting and rights would have yielded extraordinary benefits for everyone; most of all it would have improved the quality of life for those effected citizens.

The Proxy Vote for Minors may not yet be understood as important, but it runs completely in parallel to these earlier issues. It is difficult to perceive because we are not accustomed to viewing the world this way, but until children are fairly represented, their needs will be deprioritized. Full Stop. They may receive eloquent lip service, deeply expressed concern and many individuals and organizations will honestly and valiantly try different initiatives, but the evidence suggests that they will not be lastingly successful until the power of the vote is applied. There is hope that citizens can understand the wasted opportunity of the past limitations in accepting all citizens' voices as equal – that we can make change without so much unnecessary loss and conflict.

> *The struggle of today is not altogether for today--it is for a vast future also.*

> —ABRAHAM LINCOLN

Sarah Grimke	1792–1873	81
Angelina Grimke	1805–1879	74
Lucy Stone	1818–1893	75
Susan B. Anthony	1820–1906	86
Elizabeth Cady Stanton	1815–1902	87

Sadly, none of these early voices and leaders for women's suffrage lived to witness the amendment

CHAPTER 4

Seeing Through a New Lens

———

THE PRIMARY OBJECTIVE OF THIS book is to communicate why making this change is urgent and important. The secondary objective is much harder to achieve - convincing at least a few readers that it is sufficiently important to personally advocate or become directly involved to support a change. Since you are still reading, there is a chance that you've found some points worth considering – though it is quite possible that you are simply open to new ideas or find this comical. This section is directed towards readers who may see value but have reservations about some of the secondary effects of making this change. The following are brief vignettes of alternative realities of the future. They offer a view to the world seen through a different and sometimes magnified lens. Some of the approaches use extreme cases which can be useful to reveal the impact of a change which may be coming in a smaller or slower way, to better reveal how variables are interrelated. In these cases, each is targeted to address a different objection or highlight the importance of creating the proxy vote. The descriptions are simply outlines and are meant to be thought starters to support the reader's own thoughts and to provide more tangible form to the issue. To get the benefit of the thought exercise, it's necessary to think, not just read through, and dwell for a moment within each scenario to consider the implications for the future of our world.

Imagine: Changing the number of minors
This first group of variations highlights the importance of the next generation to any society by considering the effect of varying the number

children in the future and varying the competence and capability of the next generation. This discussion is intended to address the U.S. citizens who view children as a burden to society and who view the reduction in the U.S. birth rate as a positive outcome.

Imagine: A nation with no children

For this scenario, assume that beginning 2022, three years from when this was written, that our culture decides that having children is too high a burden on our personal expenses and on the environment. The nation entirely stops having children and begins to move towards becoming a child-free nation. So those children that are not born are the missing cohort of citizens from that point forward. The cohort would have begun to become adults by 2040. By 2040, when our population was expected to grow to 380 Million from the current 321 Million, it instead declines to 302 M, and by 2060 instead of 417M it shrinks to 250 Million, around the population level of the United States in 1990. This assumes that immigration remains constant at the level currently planned. As a result of these changes, our foreign born population will increase from the current level of approximately 14% to 22% and then to 31% in those years, instead of growing to 19% in that time, simply from lowering the native born population.

Let's wander around the alternative versions of the nation and explore the impact of the elimination of native births.

Advantages

– Public School Savings: Beginning in 2027, we can eliminate funding for one grade of school and continue that way until all public schools are closed, perhaps leaving some few open for the immigrant population, or alternatively requiring that they pay for private education. Real estate taxes will drop since over 50% currently goes to education. The buildings and infrastructure can be sold or leased, and teachers and administrators will seek other professions or retire, possibly spiking the public pension liability problem for a time, as earlier payment of some pensions are required, but then eliminating the need to increase pensions.

- Higher Education Savings: Similarly, beginning 2040 we will no longer have U.S. minors attending universities. We can eliminate nearly all university and financial aid funding, and around 2045 we can shutter most undergraduate training, and in a few more years all graduate training. Many universities may remain open to continue teaching foreign students, but the numbers of universities will be greatly reduced along with the number of faculty who will retire or seek other professions. Global leadership in higher education will become more challenging as the scale advantages of other nations should help them easily overtake the U.S. institutions. The facilities will be repurposed. Some universities may continue as pure research organizations using endowments to fund their activities.
- Crime Rates: beginning 2035-2040, crime rates would begin to fall, since the young are involved with crime at a higher level both as victims and as perpetrators.
- Social interaction and exposure – Beginning in 2022, there will be no crying baby in the airplane or restaurant, and soon enough no child in public who can disturb your peace, no teenager making noise outside at night. This is especially important to those with sensitive nervous systems and little patience.

Disadvantages

- Real estate values will begin to decline with an accelerating pace as the population decreases, and consequently demand for housing decreases. Houses that include multiple bedrooms experience steeper declines. Over time, second homes in the recreational areas targeted to younger families should also experience steeper decline in value. Similarly, real estate in the better school districts will see a sharper decline in value since the premium that many will pay to live in better school districts will vanish.

– Social Security and Medicare payments will be reduced since the system relies on growth in the working population to continue payments. The impact of the population changes will be easy to forecast, and will require drastic cuts, beginning 2023, and increasing the cuts over time. By 2060, 39% of the population would be over 65, but by then the system would already have collapsed or be a much smaller income supplement. Most of the rest of the population will be between 40-64 and planning to retire but with no hope of receiving any social security payments. By 2087, everyone will be over 65 except for the smaller immigrant population who will eventually inherit the nation, and so there will be no way to meet social security and Medicare payments for the population that remains.

– Business and industry – businesses in various industries would need to redirect products and services or go out of business. The large parts of the economy which are directed to children, then to teens, and finally to young adults would be eliminated.

– Stock market and private business investments – the value of businesses would take a deep dive as soon as there is recognition that the nation is declining. Businesses that can operate with few local employees and that serve customers internationally would fare best. The reverse is also true –those serving U.S. based customers would face a declining market, and those that require a younger or lower cost workforce would need to move their businesses offshore. In certain sectors, the lack of a younger and lower cost workforce would result in loss of leadership position to countries who can properly staff their businesses. Technology and life sciences related businesses either exit the nation or lose world leading positions to Asia based companies.

–   Wages – Wages for many jobs begin a steady increase as the number of available workers decline and competition for workers increases. Wages related to providing elder care increase more dramatically as demand for doctors, nurses, and support staff grows disproportionate to the growth, or in this case the reduction of the size of the general population. Businesses with entry level jobs or physical labor have no alternative than to close or raise prices to compete for older workers at higher prices, or for the limited immigrant population. Landscaping, maintenance and home services, restaurants, all see substantial price increases to compete for those willing and physically able to work.

–   Income Taxes - Income tax rates increase sharply. As the workforce shrinks and with more citizens in retirement, government repayments on the debt, expenses for defense, Medicare, and other government spending must be covered by remaining workers. At the same time, the government workers who have pension plans with shorter periods to retirement will require higher pay to be retained or they will retire early to seek employment with higher wages in the private sector where demand has forced high wage increases.

–   Immigration – immigration will increase, through both legal and illegal methods. Demand for workers will raise wages which will attract immigration. Over time, the declining economy combined with higher taxes will make immigrating to the United States less attractive, but will be balanced against newly low-cost housing so this will create a new balance and possibly attract a different immigrant group than we've seen in the past, possibly more massive immigration from the most overpopulated or least developed nations.

–   Health Care – Health care will be under pressure quickly from several areas: from a higher ratio of elderly patients per healthcare professional since there will be no younger people renewing the group of healthcare professionals; from higher wages for each healthcare professional; from higher support, maintenance and services costs for hospitals and other care facilities; and due to a higher proportion of unpaid bills placing pressure on hospitals and physicians. The bills will not be paid since there will be far fewer citizens to pay Medicare taxes, so copays will need to increase, combined with higher overall costs which will cause higher defaults by elderly patients with higher Medicare copayments and lower Social Security benefits. It will be a vicious cycle to the bottom, analogous in some ways to the housing crisis cycle of 2007. Wealthy older Americans would still be able to afford care from the immigrant healthcare professionals, but the majority of older Americans would need to either forgo care or allocate remaining savings to cover the unexpected gap in Medicare.

– Innovation does not begin to diminish until 2040 and then begins a gradual decline across all areas. It's difficult to assess how the future of the U.S. affects the potential innovators who are already born; these may shift focus to how to survive in this new world, rather than how to innovate. Some of the world's best lifesaving therapies or environment improving systems that might otherwise have been discovered may be missed. Eventually, innovation in the United States comes nearly to a halt and all innovation moves to other nations.

– Military- By 2040, the military is facing a crisis on how to properly staff defense for the United States. The U.S. must quickly pull away from any direct support and defense of allies and begin to shrink the size of all armed forces. After a few years, the U.S. must reestablish a mandatory draft of older citizens and immigrants and increasingly rely on immigrant and eventually a foreign mercenary force for self-defense. A mandatory draft will only be viable for a short time since too high a percentage of population is able to get waivers either due to their employment in essential high demand roles to support the economy or deferred as physically unfit for military service.

- Culture - Entertainment industries, sports, and music would change in that same timeframe, as the missing cohort that would have come of age is not there. Sports teams may be able to continue for a brief time as aging players extend their careers and we import others. However, over time, fans may lose interest in teams composed of solely foreign-born athletes. The music industry will rely more heavily on 'classics' music from the past since new artists rarely emerge from the older group. Film receipts will decline with loss of the youth market, so the remaining film industry must redirect films to target the demands of the rest of world. Eventually the remaining industry will be replaced by other nation's film industries.

- American Culture Wars - The Culture Wars will begin to recede in the U.S. and worldwide as American Culture begins to be replaced by the mix of beliefs of the new immigrant population, since they will no longer be blending in with native born Americans. Constitutional amendments will proliferate until the nation becomes ideologically very different and not recognizable to citizens of the early 21st century.

- The World - Political ideologies and values of more aggressive and growing nations begin to become more dominant. Militarily aggressive nations note the declining ability and willingness of the U.S. to support and defend smaller democratic nations. The long term-diminishment and decline of democratic nations outside of Europe becomes nearly assured.

- Unfunded Liabilities and the National Debt - The unfunded liabilities would naturally never be paid, since the ability to continue to increase taxes to catch up with these would be impossible. The unfunded liabilities issue may never be visible, because when the nation's decline becomes assured, it will become impossible to fund the National Debt, causing a broader economic collapse.

This example used an extreme change to that one dimension, the birth rate, to make more visible some of the secondary effects of changes on that dimension. In this case, a reduction to zero would obviously destine a society to diminishment and finally to virtual extinction. Immigration is the only method of preventing complete extinction in that case. Although it is extreme, its value lies in highlighting the effect of diminishing numbers of children in future generations. It would be very difficult to determine the formulaic relationship between the level of population growth and the impact on each separate aspect of society, but it is more probably exponential than linear. For example, the U.S. national fertility rate of 1.86 births per woman in 2013,[82] (U.S. Department of Health and Human Services, 2017) is below the replacement rate of 2.07, but when immigration is included the U.S. continues to grow. If that fertility rate were to drop to 1.0 births per woman, some of the items above may change only slightly, while others may still change more dramatically. For example, wages may change only slightly, since there may be alternative ways to combine automation, artificial intelligence, visiting workers, and immigration to reduce the impact. Other areas, for example the impact on leadership in innovation, on shared values of the nation, or on social security funding, may have a much higher, more exponential effect as the rate decreases.

Imagine: Double the number of children
In the last scenario, we considered how reducing the number of children would impact several areas of our society. It was an extreme example, but with a little imagination, it becomes obvious that it would not be a good world to live in, despite the elimination of the noisy-child airplane or restaurant experiences. Lesser versions of this would carry a lesser deterioration and the leverage points and relative proportional effects are not easy to determine. In this section, we wander through the opposite world, where we double the number of births from the 2015 rate 1.86 to 3.72 (compared to 2018 of 1.72), nearly the same as when it reached a peak in the late 1950's. (Please keep in mind that in

this section we are just thinking - this is an example to contrast directional effects, NOT a recommendation that the government promote a higher birth rate!). Let's explore this alternative future....

Most of the changes will be the mirror image of the example of no children:

Advantages

– Real estate values will continue to increase, possibly with an accelerating pace as the population increases and with a long-term expectation of increased demand for a growing population. The additional demand will require increased building and increased employment in the construction, materials, and large appliance sectors. Houses that include multiple bedrooms and those with better school districts will experience steeper increases. Vacation homes in recreational areas targeted to younger families should also experience a steeper increase in value.

– Social Security and Medicare payments into the system will continue to grow. In the near term, families will need to increase income to support their larger families. Over the longer term, the growth in the population will return the nation to more of a pyramidal distribution, moving towards resolving the shortfalls in funding, allowing continuation of payments. This will provide the opportunity for the system to be adjusted to ensure that it does not rely on continued growth to be self-supporting.

– Stock market and private business investments – The value of businesses would increase in anticipation of continued long-term growth in the U.S., with increasing long-term demand in domestic markets. The growth in a young workforce should continue to fuel innovation in technology, life sciences, and healthcare.

– Business and industry – Most industries would see an increase in demand. The large parts of the economy which are directed to children, teens, and young adults would receive the most benefit, but many other sectors that serve those businesses would also benefit. The additional spiking demand for education will support increased focus on bringing economically sound educational technology to education.

- Wages – Wages will be determined by the relative growth in the economy compared to the number of new workers coming on board. The historic success in the U.S. of creating new products and entire new industries suggests that wages will continue to increase as long as there is continued drive towards creating new ways to serve U.S. and world consumers.

- Income Taxes – Similarly, the gross level of income tax rates will be determined by the number of workers and their overall income. With a growing economy, it should be possible to allow rates to stabilize or for the rates to decrease, but still have an increase in the national funding through GDP growth.

- Immigration – Decisions about immigration can be taken independent of the need for new workers. The nation can continue to refresh itself through the addition of immigrants who bring new energy and are motivated by ambition or personal need, in a proportion that does not overwhelm or concern the nation's current citizens. The continuing growth of the existing population will allow higher numbers of immigrants to arrive without dramatically increasing the proportion of immigrant population.

- Health Care – Medicare funding will be safer with a larger young population to support the commitments already made to date. A larger young population will be available to work in health care and life sciences industries, possibly supporting greater innovation and possibly life extending or enhancing treatments that improve the lives of the elderly.

- Innovation - Innovation begins to show even further increase around 2040 and then continues to increase across all areas as the growing next generation begins to contribute. The United States takes a more dominant role in international innovation as the other economically and technologically advanced nations continue with declining birth rates and their funding continues to shift to support the health issues of their increasingly elderly populations.

- Military - The military continues attracting dedicated personnel into service. The U.S. continues to support and assist in the defense of its friends and allies and the potential application of that force continues to at least somewhat dissuade the more aggressive nations from their imperial objectives.

- American Culture Wars - The Culture Wars will need to change as young Americans become annoyed by the intransigence of the many diverse groups and organizations pulling in separate ways. People in power who attempt to pull the culture further apart will become more marginalized and lose their leadership positions. A greater recognition of the importance of protecting children and young minds may lead to a renewal of respect for others, reemergence of etiquette, empathy and compassion. Sometimes the young can have a clearer perspective from having observed the prior generation's egregious behavior when the adults thought they were too young to understand. Maybe they can end the horrible vitriol and divisiveness. Maybe not, but we can hope.

- The World – The political ideologies and plans of the more aggressive nations begin to recede as they struggle with their internal issues of declining birthrates and dissatisfied population (yearning to breathe free). Militarily aggressive nations note the increasing technological advantage and commitment to freedom of the U.S. and begin to reign in their expansionist plans and seek better ways to improve their own citizen's situations.

Disadvantages

- Public School Costs: Beginning in 2027, school funding will need to increase as each grade of school requires more teachers or alternative teaching methods to support the increase in students. Over time, new buildings or additional infrastructure will be needed. Technology that assists in the process of teaching and the process of learning may provide leverage for current staff and allow leverage of existing facilities.
- Higher Education Costs: Similarly, beginning 2040 the U.S. will require additional capacity within universities and other forms of post-secondary education.
- Crime Rates: beginning 2035-2040, crime rates may begin to increase, since the young are involved with crime at a higher level both as victims and as perpetrators. Since there is substantial time to plan for this, there is some hope that improvements in how the nation's children are supported, and how new opportunities are presented to all citizens, can mitigate or prevent the growth in crime.
- Social interaction and exposure – Beginning in 2022, there will be additional crying babies in airplanes and restaurants, and extra children in public who will disturb your peace. Soon enough, extra teenagers making noise at night. This is especially important to those with sensitive nervous systems and little patience. New noise cancelling headsets and new ways to separate will be created for the especially sensitive or persnickety adults.

The economy gains many benefits through growth. An aware observer would recognize that much of an economy is like a gargantuan pyramid scheme where values depend on expectations of long-term future returns. It is not a pyramid scheme, but rather the correct way to assess value – based on long term future returns. So growth is good, and nearly essential. We rely directly on growth to fund future payments of Social Security and Medicare. Our stock markets values are built on expectations of growth and all real estate values are a function of future need for that real estate, with only a small portion of the value related to near term use. The value of the dollar, all financial instruments, gold, art, the value of pension plans, and everything in the economy which can be considered an investment, are all based on expectations; everything of financial value is indirectly affected by the level of growth and future demand.

Beyond the direct economic areas, the most interesting area to examine is the effect of the additional people on innovation. It's self-evident that a networking effect occurs in science and technology. It can be clearly seen in the development and continuous renewal of Silicon Valley, as well as in many similar centers of technology development throughout the U.S. and the world. The technology ecosystem builds on the interaction of people, knowledge, and ideas – with teams and some individuals who develop the next set of ideas from the platform or foundation of a predecessor's effort. One might think: 'Is each person really necessary?' What is the effect of one more or less? One can argue that if there was no Steve Jobs, Bill Gates, Larry Page, Sergey Brin, Larry Ellison, or Jeff Bezos, that someone would have eventually provided the world with the same products and services. It's impossible to know, but it's likely that eventually a very similar idea or solution would be developed. One can argue that removing one individual would not stop the innovation and that the person could be replaced by others, but it is not credible to argue that others would have done it at the same time. It is not credible to argue that one could remove many people of that caliber and not experience a much slower pace in innovation. That slower innovation would have a negative impact on the economy and the compounding benefits that the world has enjoyed over the last century.

If we removed half of those individuals, the pace of innovation in their related areas will probably slow by more than half. We can think of the increase in the amount of innovation simply as either more than linear or less than linear to population. It is impossible to know or study this empirically. There are too many uncontrollable variables to study so there is no way to have a control group. But the evidence of the past 50 years suggests that innovations build upon each other and compound; innovations build upon other prior innovations, so each step forward provides a boost to the next step. One example that was experienced by many in the Baby Boomer generation was the introduction of IBM's personal computer in 1982. Other companies were already offering microcomputers, but that introduction fired up the industry in software and hardware development towards development of a broader industry, along with the seeds of other entirely new industry sectors. Had the personal computer industry taken a year longer to ramp due to delayed introduction at IBM, there may have been a delay in innovations in semiconductor technology with slower volume ramps, a delay in software development through lower demand, and magnified across other areas within tech; not just in that industry, but also across so many other disciplines. The power of the personal computer supported individuals in many disciplines in their research and development activities, as did many other capability expanding developments which followed. Remove just a few people from the development or business teams and the effect ripples across the world.

Doubling the number of children would also have implications for the environment, and compounding effects when extended beyond the first generation. A comprehensive discussion of human impact on the planet is beyond the scope of this discussion. Although it is too deep to wade in fully, there are reasons to believe that deterioration of the environment would not result.

First, that the young have a longer-term perspective and have shown leadership in highlighting environmental issues. Second, our society has done well in remediating bad environmental practices. The clearest empirical evidence of properly adjusting our collective behaviors to act as good stewards comes from the improvements in air quality as a result of the Clean Air Act. The Clean Air Act was signed into law in 1970, and important amendments were added in 1990 to address ozone depletion and acid rain. Since 1970, the U.S. has reduced six common pollutants (particles, ozone, lead, carbon monoxide, nitrogen dioxide and sulfur dioxide) by 70 percent while the gross domestic product increased by 246 percent.[83] (Environmental Protection Agency) There were innovations applied in the auto, energy, and power industries throughout the industrial U.S. to achieve this result.

Another issue which is difficult to address in the doubling of the birth rate scenario is the impact to daily lives. For many adults, the idea of growing the number of children may seem quite annoying or distasteful. It is an interesting dichotomy that many people express - the contrast of high enjoyment, tolerance, and concern for our own children and those of our extended family and in our personal network, vs. the much lower concern, ranging down to beyond dislike for the children of others. This may simply be the result of Darwinian evolution, since under conditions of limited resources, humans protected their own extended family and chased off or killed the other group, to the advantage of the genes of their group in the next generation. Sounds awful, doesn't it!? As awful as it sounds, it may explain some commonly repeating opinions and behaviors. Maybe it would be helpful if we also consciously repeated the mantra that all humankind is the same family and view the children of others as related to us.

If these behaviors stem from some past evolutionary advantage that lead to our current behavior, in today's world they are certainly as obsolete as our cravings for excessive calories and should be recognized and discouraged, and never spoken in public. They lead us to behaviors that are the reverse of what is good for us or good for the world. Our neighbor's children are not a burden or drag on our future; they instead create a better future for us. That child born today may conduct the critical research that leads to a therapy that extends your life or the life of someone you love. They could write the novel or explain the philosophy or paint the picture that gives you peace or insight or pleasure. The children are additive. It is not a zero-sum game. The fact that

Steve Jobs became rich did not make us poor – he led innovation which fueled other areas. It is not a zero-sum game! His personal wealth, coming from personal efforts, eventually becomes his children's wealth and over generations' returns into the world. It is not a zero-sum game!!

Imagine: Valuing the nation's children as the most cherished investments

By excluding minors from representation, democratic nations have neglected proper support of the highest returning investment that we can make – in that of young citizens at a critical point in life. For many citizens, the view of a human being as valuable and worthy as an investment is a given, but for others there is a need for these repeated reminders, which is the reason for this entire section. A refresher on simple examples of good investments:

* Planting a crop or a tree –It takes very little investment to plant a seed and provide fertilizer and irrigation. With a limited additional investment, the outcome is likely to be even better. Humankind's move from hunter-gatherers to farmers allowed our ancestors to move from basic subsistence societies to societies that can develop, and with sufficient resources to progress and innovate. Mankind collectively owes much to the simple investment idea of planting seeds. Plant a tree or some vegetables and you'll find that there is an amazing return on your investment.

* Financial investments - Most people recognize that having money to invest in the stock market, a bond, a business or a miserably low returning, but safe, CD is smart and good and may give you options in the future.

* Investment in other people – The emergence of banking structures and financial instruments allowed people to loan or invest in each other, providing better returns. The venture capital system that developed within the technology sector and fueled the

amazing innovation of the past 60 years has expanded the world for all of us.

❖   Investment in children - For most of human history, societies perceived the same of the investment in children and in the extended family and community. Financial wealth and personal security could be supported by raising children and belonging to a large family. This idea crosses cultures and many centuries.

With the view that investing in the young is the best return on investment, it is a poor investment decision to neglect allowing them to be represented. The vote is not about a redistribution of wealth. As discussed earlier, there is a broad range of societal actions that the vote influences, and the broader factors have large implications for children.

Malthus and the Misanthropes in Humanitarian Clothing

There is a line of thinking that competes with the view of the young as a great investment. In the various versions of that thinking, the next human on earth is not an investment at all, but rather a cost, a heavy burden, excess population or worse, as a destructive entity that must be prevented. The associated concern is that humanity is a burden on the earth; that we will soon use up all of the resources and that Mother Earth will be forever damaged. The various flavors of this trumpet openly that the next child is a burden and that it is virtuous to help prevent their birth. The belief that we are reaching the earth's capacity to sustain the population has long existed but was first codified as a scholarly viewpoint by Thomas Malthus, an English cleric and demographic and economics scholar, in 1798. His efforts were presumably well intentioned when his book, *An Essay on the Principle of Population* was first published anonymously in 1798, predicting a grim future of geometric global population growth and arithmetic food production growth. The book predicted the inevitable result of terrible suffering through mass starvation. His words from 1798: *"The power of population is indefinitely greater than the power in the earth to produce subsistence for man"*

In early civilizations, that statement was true. The population was limited by readily accessible resources, beginning with limited fertile and arable land, combined with limited knowledge and technology, in this case the technology was primitive farming tools. If the population grew, farming extended into more marginal land until the additional land no longer sustained the additional population. These limitations assured that any increasing population was temporary. It would inevitably lead to declining health and income, until a famine would finally bring the population back to a sustainable level. The oversight in Malthus's analysis may have been that he relied on the results of the centuries prior to his own to develop his perspectives. Although prior centuries did demonstrate this cycle of reaching a peak population followed by famine, then population decline coincident with an increase in per capita income - by his century this theory was already no longer valid. Beginning early in the 18th century, Great Britain was overcoming those old limits through improvements in farming and manufacturing technologies, demonstrating rapid and consistent improvements in productivity and yield.

The evidence of the century following Malthus repeatedly proved that his forecast of catastrophic events was not valid; the exact opposite was proved true, with simultaneous gains in per capita income and population. Nevertheless, even today we continue to hear the same concepts repeated in different forms and using different but similar disaster scenarios, some repeated in different groups among the current anti-child or child-free movements. Sadly, this includes some of the professional environmentalists. More recently, in the 1968 best-selling book The Population Bomb, written by Paul Ehrlich, a professor at one of our most esteemed universities, Stanford University, predictions of mass starvation due to overpopulation were once again confidently broadcast as a highly certain threat. In this case, the doomsayer showed great courage compared to so many other doom predictors, by forecasting the doom close enough in time so the results could be observed during his lifetime. The predictions, were bold, stated with certainty, and enormously bleak:[84] (Ehrlich, 1968)

"The battle to feed all of humanity is over. In the 1970s hundreds of millions of people will starve to death in spite of any crash programs embarked upon now. At this late date nothing can prevent a substantial increase in the world death rate."

In 1970: *"in ten years all important animal life in the sea will be extinct."*

In 1971: *"By the year 2000 the United Kingdom will be simply a small group of impoverished islands, inhabited by some 70 million hungry people."*

From Wikipedia: "He suggests a tax scheme in which additional children would add to a family's tax burden at increasing rates for more children, as well as luxury taxes on childcare goods. He suggests incentives for men who agree to permanent sterilization before they have two children, as well as a variety of other monetary incentives. He proposes a powerful Department of Population and Environment which "should be set up with the power to take whatever steps are necessary to establish a reasonable population size in the United States and to put an end to the steady deterioration of our environment." The department should support research into population control, such as better contraceptives, mass sterilizing agents, and prenatal sex discernment (because families often continue to have children until a male is born. Ehrlich suggested that if they could choose a male child this would reduce the birthrate, effectively calling for the abortion of most female fetuses).

The list of doomsayer predictions from Dr. Ehrlich continued from that time to the near present day. Despite being so obviously and repeatedly wrong through most of the last 50 years, Dr. Ehrlich has continued to repeat variations on the same mantra, written at least 17 books and been highly honored with a similar number of major awards, primarily from the leading environmental groups. He still contends that governments should discourage people from having more than two children, suggesting, for example a greater tax rate for larger families.

There is a reason to highlight these forecasts and the ultimate results, because very similar theories continue to be put forth by many prominent and well-meaning politicians, celebrities, academics, royalty, and other influential people. The ideas and principles that are espoused by these groups and their proposals are the antithesis of what would result through Authentic Democracy and the proxy vote which would make it less onerous to raise a family and lend society's support to raising and fully developing children.

The world population has more than doubled since the highly honored Mr. Ehrlich wrote the first predictions of our doom. The predictions are not simply refuted by the facts, but the results have proven nearly directly the opposite of his theories as evidenced by empirical data.[85] (Ortiz-Ospina, 2017) Global extreme poverty has moved from 94% of the population in 1820, (meaning most of us have ancestors coming from poverty at that time), to around 25% in 2000, to 9.9%[86] in 2015 and continuing to decline. Population is growing more slowly than in the past, though it is not yet level. The fear of insufficient land and productivity has been essentially eliminated. Fully 31% of the world's land area is suitable for crops, but only 11% is currently in use for crop production.[87] (Food and Agriculture Organization of the United Nations) [89] At the same time, yields and productivity continue to increase, For example, corn grain yields have moved from about 20 bushels per acre in 1870 to 140 in 2000, to nearly 180 in 2016. Similar results are seen in other staple foods categories. For two centuries, employment in agriculture has continued to decline while supplying more food per consumer, to an increasing population.

This concern about insufficient resources is not a new fear. On the contrary, it is an ancient and recurring concern, only now it is more sophisticated and scientific sounding in its description. It is a simple fear - that the tribe, village, group, nation or world is running out of resources; that the limit has been reached and it is a worldwide zero-sum game. This has been a driver of wars and genocide, to ensure that there will be enough resources for each favored group. You can just hear the pagan priest requiring the sacrifice of many virgins to the gods or to the sun, to ensure a good rain or a good harvest or enough heat. Remember that to those villagers, the pagan priest was the smartest, most educated man and seemed to have an insider's knowledge of how things worked, and he had a very sophisticated story for his time. He was very convincing and could explain the connections. (How many times and in how many forms has this happened during human civilization?) Why does this repeat itself so often and coming from the educated subset of the intelligentsia? It may simply be a natural evolutionary instinct to look ahead for greater resources with some fear – then unconsciously convert this into an intellectual explanation by smart guys who explain to other smart guys who agree wholeheartedly that this is an important thing. It's not clear what it is, but it's as old as the hills.

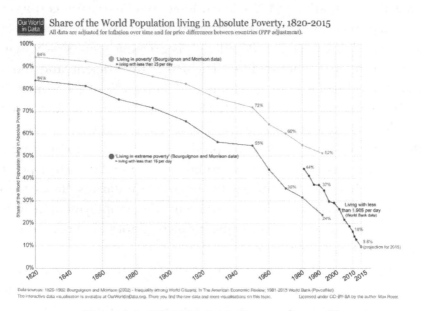

Share of the World Living in Extreme Poverty[88]

The point here is not to challenge that the environment should be protected; it must be. The nation should be grateful that the environmental movement began powerfully and was recognized widely as essential to the future. But the extreme beliefs that view humans not as an investment in the future, but as a burden on the earth is not only flawed, but foolish and is a form of misanthropy. It is misanthropy in stealth mode, stated as a virtue.

To make this more concrete, it may be useful to conduct another simple thought experiment. The world population recently crossed 7.5 Billion people in 2017. For the experiment, we can consider what the world might be like if we were to arbitrarily roll it back to a more idyllic 2.5 Billion, the approximate world population in 1950. The test is to support the hypothesis that the investment in the other 5 Billion was well worth it, not just for the 5 Billion people themselves who now have a life, but even for the 2.5 Billion who this experiment would have allowed to live.

Let's mentally run the experiment and consider some of the results. Fortunately, we have some simple data to run a thought experiment. Let's take a group of prominent people, here focusing on a group of the technology innovators born since 1950 and consider how the world might be different if 2/3 of them had not been born. The group of innovators and contributors in these industries is more like tens of thousands, but these are some fairly well-known names for the exercise:

1	Jeff Bezos	1964	Amazon, Blue Origin, etc.
2	Steve Jobs	1955	
3	Steve Wozniak	1950	Apple etc.
4	Tim Cook	1960	
5	Bill Gates	1955	Microsoft
6	Paul Allen	1953	
7	Michael Dell	1965	Dell
8	Marc Benioff	1964	Salesforce
9	Elon Musk	1971	Tesla, PayPal, etc.
10	Larry Page	1973	Alphabet/Google, etc.
11	Sergey Brin	1973	
12	Mark Zuckerberg	1984	Facebook

Pick your own way to eliminate the 2/3 or 8 – e.g. 1) keeping the first and eliminate the next two, all the way through; 2) or keep the first 4 and eliminate the rest; or 3) just pick your favorite 4 to keep or least favorite 4; or 4) the first 4 birth years. Whichever way that you choose, the world falls substantially behind its current position in technology from their removal. If 2/3 of these technology leaders (and let's bring along 2/3 of the contributors in the rest of the population) had not been born, the companies which they founded would not exist and it's highly likely that many other new companies would also not exist. Much of innovation and human development builds upon what predecessors and peers have already developed, and since innovation builds across industry boundaries (computing power helps science experiments and trade transactions), think about the other consequences. A wild guess on where we'd be is to estimate that if 2/3 of the people-years of innovation since 1950 was eliminated, we'd be at the equivalent of 1982 in technology. Maybe 1990, but certainly not where we are today. Not just from these few, but consider all of the other 2/3 of contributors. This group of innovators is in the high-tech sectors of computers, software, internet, and social media, but the same way of looking at this subgroup could be applied to any group, like winners of the Nobel Prize for Peace or Medicine or Physics. Many of the innovations in medicines, medical technologies, energy production, environmental sciences, farming technologies, etc. would be diminished by a third. We might have the Beatles, but we'd have to give up the Rolling Stones and The Who; we might have the Four Tops, but we'd have to give up the Supremes and Marvin Gaye; we might keep Ed Sheeran, but we'd have to give up Adele and Sam Smith.

Civilization progresses based on collective progress, building on top of the prior without requiring a formal intervention. The adoption of technologies and knowledge defuses across the world, at increasing speeds – now extremely rapidly when compared to all prior human history. The importance and value of the contributions gets more personal if you or someone you love has had the need for modern medicines or a medical procedure. The difference in availability of procedures over the last 50 years in the United States has been remarkable. You may be aware of the level of benefit that each of us receives in every area through a large and dynamic world. If you regularly use a computer, a smartphone, or the internet, you have used the benefit of a compounding of the innovation.

The final part of this thought experiment makes it a little more personal. If we must eliminate 2/3 of the population, we must not only decide what might be missing from those who were not born, but we must decide if we ourselves are eliminated. Take a coin and flip it twice. If you get heads twice, you survived. If not, you are out (actually this gives 25% not 33%, but close enough to preserve the simplicity of the step).

Humans are of benefit to each other. A better world comes about through valuing the lives of the next human, not seeing them as a burden. Authentic Democracy and representation of minor citizens would provide the support needed by young families to continue to have children and allow them to develop to the benefit of all citizens. We don't need to create incentives or have the government involved in promoting births, we must simply make the society a little more supportive for young citizens by allowing the vote.

Be fruitful and multiply, and fill the earth

GENESIS 1:28

This phrase from Genesis can be interpreted in many ways, and some are controversial. If you are not religious or not of the Abrahamic religions, it may seem meaningless or a cynical person might believe it was conceived as a manipulation by an ambitious leader to promote procreation to grow the community for the leader's benefit. For others it is read as a command to have as many children as possible. It is ambiguous in this English translation and may be clearer in the original language. Regardless of the interpretation, the concept of producing – children, crops, buildings, etc. is fundamental to civilization – and that viewpoint is fundamental to a healthy and progressing society. Rightly so, because it is the best way to contribute to one's fellow man. When we produce more than we consume during a lifetime, we leave something behind which contributes to the world. The simplest and most direct reading of the Genesis quote is as wise guidance about how to live a useful and happy life.

Humanity has often made the mistake of believing that the current era is a new age of the wisest and best, i.e., look how much knowledge and insight we have compared to my parent's time or the past generations of humanity. However, many aspects of human life are much the same as they were in the past. Much of life is easier, with science, medicine, technology, human rights, and wealth all improving. However, it's not so clear that wisdom comes from scientific knowledge, nor through access to information, or wealth, or through an easier lifestyle. It may be more correct that wisdom comes from overcoming adversity, and certainly our predecessors faced and overcame more adversity than the subsequent generations. Wisdom and compassion may come from interacting with others in deeper relationships through a community, and in the deeper thought that comes from reading and writing, both areas long in decline. So if we are not wiser now, than perhaps we should be more careful about dismissing the fundamental building blocks of modern civilization, and instead reinforce the commitment to them - support from the community for families with children, valuing the contribution of families and the growth of children - instead of viewing them as a burden, or worse, as a threat to the environment.

Imagine: World's best performance in education

Imagine the nation moving from its current mediocre performance to become the world leader in primary and secondary education. The implications for the nation's long-term future would be somewhere between truly promising to exceptional. The economic benefits of an excellent education are obvious – but the importance of an excellent education extends well beyond economic benefits. The higher and shared level of knowledge should create more understanding and shared values, fostering the common bonds necessary for a cohesive society. A shared basic grounding in history, science, mathematics, economics, health, and most of the disciplines among the liberal arts will enhance the student's quality of life for a lifetime and foster the shared experience necessary to cohesive culture.

The foundation which education provides has direct economic benefits for individuals and broadly to the community. We know that the importance and need for advanced education will increase as our technology increases, with new tools which allow greater leverage of each individual's potential and reach. Anticipating a future where we move from our current level of educational quality to world leading performance, what should we expect? As that generation applies their better knowledge, their innovation and better overall performance, everything is affected in the same way as described in the growth scenario above, increasing stock value, real estate, the value of other investments, etc. Conversely – children provided with poor education will inevitably lose in global competition, as globalization continues to lead inevitably to a more competitive environment. In a competitive environment, where others will be willing to do the work necessary to achieve excellence, we can lose by simply not attempting to be excellent. The status quo in education will lead to inevitable decline.

The rest of the world has a growing middle class with education vastly improved from their recent past. Globalization brings them to our doorstep to compete with the children in our local schools. The U.S. has 4% of the population, and a smaller percentage of the world's children, so every U.S. child will be competing with 24 or more peers across the world. The current trend makes it clear that the U.S. cannot remain on the current system and expect anything other than eventual decline in its leadership in many areas. There are objective measures of U.S. national performance which demonstrate that under no circumstance should we view the current performance as a world leading position. In fact, the results lead citizens to question whether the system is providing a fair return for what is invested.

The list of statistics that demonstrate major gaps in performance is long, but two are repeated here to support the point, though it may already be generally accepted. In a nationally representative sample of high school seniors at 740 schools, the results showed a relative lack of proper preparation for the level expected in the grade. Only 37 percent demonstrated readiness for college level math and reading, though 69 percent of students proceed to college. Only 25 percent tested as proficient in math.[89] (National Assessment of Nations Progress) Consistent with this, in the premier international survey of 15-year olds worldwide, the Programme for International Student Assessment tests (PISA,) the United States continues to perform well behind the leading performers. In the 2015 PISA tests of 540,000 students, the U.S. ranked 25th in science, and 40th in math. There are always objections to the methodology and explanations for such mediocre results in each study, but the fact is that we are not performing well, and the system is not meeting the objective.

Imagine: Alternative rules to define voting eligibility
This imagine step addresses the inevitable objection that will be advanced that since the children have not contributed to society yet, they should not be represented with a vote. Following that logic path takes us down some bizarre alternative realities, some of which are systems that the world has tried and already well discarded.

* Contribution as a requirement for the vote - This is consistent with the rules of an aristocracy or oligarchy, where wealth, class, landownership, or birthright is a requirement for the franchise and for political power. The poll tax was a similar version of these screens. We've already soundly rejected this concept. Outside of the direct voting process, many areas of contribution can continue to have influence on how others vote and on

representatives, but the vote itself remains pure to the concept of one citizen per vote (except for now, excluding minor citizens). The wealthy, smart, famous, or attractive can continue to use their money or argument or fame or charm to try to influence the election, but the vote remains pure to one vote to one citizen.

❋ Time as a citizen – One could imagine an argument that a minor has not been a citizen long enough to deserve to be considered or to have a representative voice in the future of the nation. Similar to the argument above that a certain contribution is necessary for vote, this would suggest that since minors have been citizens for a very short time, they have not yet 'earned' the right of citizenship. That same logic would then need to be applied to immigrants, which would be a substantial change to the long established idea that we welcome immigration and grant full citizenship reasonably quickly. It also returns to the suggestion of having to contribute a certain amount of something, in this case time as a citizen, before receiving voting power, which has no logical basis. Lastly, it conflicts logically with the roles we elect representatives to execute. Although some of the work of government representatives relates to policy decisions that affect the near term, most policy decisions have a greater impact on the longer term future. With that in mind, the consideration of time remaining as a citizen is certainly as important as time as a citizen. Since a citizen at 85 has a life expectancy of 6 additional years, and a 10 year old has a life expectancy of 79 additional years, the young citizen has 13 times the future years ahead as a citizen. This doesn't suggest that a 10-year-old citizen receive 13 times the voting power of the 85-year-old, but their interest in the policy decisions of the nation should surely be recognized.

Instead of any conditions on the vote, retaining the purity of an equal vote for each citizen ensures that there is nothing another can do to limit any person's equality by creating artificial conditions to determine eligibility. It allows every citizen to attempt to optimize the world towards their freedom and pursuit of happiness.

Imagine: A world without consumer choice
This vignette seeks to highlight the performance deterioration which happens when consumer choice is removed from the equation for any product or service. It highlights that without a vote, minors and their representatives are disconnected from the power needed to exercise choice in the decisions of government which most affect them. For this exercise, we'll explore the government taking a monopoly position over a major portion of our daily lives. As a brief refresher on terms, when a group has exclusive control and possession of a commodity or service, that is called a monopoly.

For this scenario, imagine that the government takes over responsibility for providing our food. We are assigned to a local area government cafeteria to attend each day for breakfast, lunch, and dinner. The workers in the cafeteria are well paid and the vast majority have tenure, with a strong union with national level resources to deal with any local consumer insurrection. As a result, most consumers conclude that they have limited influence over making significant change. Although there is a local food board, they are incomparably overmatched in size and scale by entrenched powers in the food establishment and in the workers union.

Consider how the quality of the food and the selection of alternatives will compare to what you would select from the supermarket if you were permitted a choice. Or how it would compare to a local restaurant which you could chose to attend or chose not to attend. If you are a captive consumer, and the power of the workers and union is high, how much effort would you expend to try to personally improve the system compared to the alternative of spending your own money to seek an alternative? Which groups would be most captive and unable to seek the alternative? (Perhaps the poor and those who have a difficult work schedule, like working families?)

Corporations with a monopoly position serving captive consumers can lower the quality of their offering and extract higher prices from their captive customers. It is the perfect situation for the monopolist who can determine their optimal balance of service and price to maximize the profits that come to them; generally, they lower service levels and float the price upwards. All the while, the monopolist will state that they are providing the best possible service that is cost effective. They will sound sincere, sometimes they come to believe it. They will be enraged at the claim that they are not providing the best service, regardless of quantifiable data that proves the opposite. The same exists in the offering of government services. The argument that all workers are dedicated professionals, which is often used, is just a great head fake, and is simply changing the subject. The workers can be sincere, kind, hardworking, and dedicated professionals, and at the same time they are exercising their monopoly power by keeping their customers captive, delivering lower quality than they would be required to in a free market, and extracting higher rents and compensation. They can do so directly and indirectly, and it's proven to work well through the combination of the union alignment with selected politicians to ensure ease of negotiation. This is ultimately the behavior of any government institution providing services to citizens, for the same reason it occurs with corporations. Since the citizen or customer has no choice, control and power is held by the provider of the service.

As citizens, the only power to combat the monopoly of government services is through representation through elected representatives. This would be the highest impact area of the proxy – forcing the attention of our elected representatives more directly on the citizens who are most affected by their decisions. The top four areas of State and local spending, comprising 61% of spending are 1) Elementary and secondary education; 2. Public Welfare; 3. Higher Education; 4. Health and Hospitals. Each has a very direct impact on that group of minors. Completely excluding their input from decisions ensures that the systems will never properly address their needs.

Imagine: Our nation if women and minorities had never received the power to vote

This one is unpleasant to ruminate on for long, but it's a useful exercise. The reason to explore this nightmare scenario is to expand thinking about the power and importance of the vote and the full franchise and its broader impact on the culture. For this scenario, imagine that the rest of the world outside the U.S. has continued with social progress in the way that it has to date – some moving quickly and others slowly. Assume also that none of the of key franchise amendments to the Constitution were passed including the 19th Amendment signed in 1920 which prohibited states and the federal government from denying the right to vote on the basis of sex, and the Voting Rights Act of 1965 which included numerous regulations to protect the voting rights of minorities, already technically provided in the 14th Amendment of 1868 defining equal protection and citizenship and 15th Amendment prohibiting state and federal governments from denying the right to vote based on "race, color, or previous condition of servitude".

It is not pleasant to wander this world, but let's do a quick scan and leave quickly:

–   There would be a lower workforce participation rate in employment especially for women and a much lower wage rate. There are past and current census figures that can support an estimate of the impact, but forecasting the impact of change requires some assumptions and back-of-the-envelope estimates. For example, in 1920, women comprised 20% of the employed population, with very few in managerial or executive level positions. By 2016, women's portion of the labor population moved to 46% or 49.1 M of the 111.1 full time employees, with far more penetration into professional and executive positions. For this simple simulation, assume that without the change in the franchise, other aspects of our society would have similarly stagnated. Returning women's participation rate to 20%, without including the other assumed changes in compensation, eliminates the contribution of 33.7M women or $1.3M Trillion annually in wages. This change would shrink the U.S. economy, removing fully 28% of total wages. Naturally, this would have begun some time ago, so there would be a compounding effect from the original time. One would also wonder how not passing the 19th amendment might have reduced the number of women in the factories during World War II and the implications for the outcome of the war, along with the ability of the U.S. to support the Marshall plan to assist Europe's economic recovery after WWII. There is a compounding effect here that goes on and on. The world would be very different, and in no way would it be good.

– The same exercise of economic impact would apply to the vote affecting minorities, though more dramatically. It would be much more complex to calculate, but it seems obvious enough that the calculations above should provide a sense of proportion. The experience of African American, Asian American and different Hispanic populations varies greatly, but the results would be similar - the nation would lose a dramatically large portion of its progress over the last 150 years.

– Without these amendments and the voting rights act, it's not likely the 1965 Immigration and Nationality Act removing national origin quotas would have passed, so a large portion of the 12.5 M Asian immigrants and their U.S. born children would not be here. This group makes a relatively high contribution to the economy compared to the general population with a higher median income per household compared to other immigrants and native born citizens. For example, in 2014, Asian Immigrants had a median income of $70,000, compared to $49,000 for other immigrants and $55,000 for native born Americans. Asian immigrants also achieve higher levels of education with over 50% holding bachelor degrees, compared to 29% for the overall immigrant population and 30% for all native born citizens.[90] (Batalova, 2016) Beyond the direct impact of their employment, Asian immigrants have contributed extensively to innovation and business formation within technology and the sciences, most notably within Silicon Valley, and helped enable extending that ecosystem to supporting nations in Asia, extending U.S. power as a global economy.

– The most obvious national economic impact will come from the reduction in innovation since without the vote, there would likely be continuation of other discriminatory practices, so we must assume the removal of the many innovations contributed by women, minorities, and immigrants across all areas. Some smaller subset would continue to contribute just as some number did before the franchise, but it would be much diminished since they would generally continue to be relegated to lesser roles.

– Women in Science and Technology - Creating a measure for the impact is difficult, but assuming that lack of the vote would discourage other societal changes, the scale of change can be framed by examining the participation of women in select STEM disciplines: Med school graduates - 47.6% in 2015; 49.8% of enrolled med students in 2016. Engineering – 19% of bachelors; 23% of graduate degrees in 2011. Biological sciences – 59.6% of bachelors; 56.6% of graduate degrees in 2011. Math and Computer Science – 25% of bachelors; 41% of graduate degrees. These might all have remained a fraction of these levels.

– Quality of life for women, African Americans, Asian Americans and other minorities in the U.S. - Had these amendments not passed, the quality of life in the U.S. would be intolerable for any disenfranchised group to accept. The nation would be in continuous turmoil, since the fight for the franchise would dominate national politics. Beyond that, most households would be in turmoil as injustice wreaks havoc upon everyone. As the rest of the world continued to become more enlightened, more just and more inclusive, the contrast would be increasingly stark and finally the United States would stand strangely alone. With the economy deteriorating and a low quality of life, women and minorities would increasingly emigrate to other nations. The U.S. would be a bleak and unfortunate country that squandered the original dream. For the LGBT community, we would still be in the dark ages.

– Life for white males – With the exception of a very few individuals, this nation would not be a place acceptable for the white males of 21st century America. There are always exceptions, but what may have seemed normal in 1820 or 1920, would be recognized now as criminal, wrong, unjust, or cruel. Very few would want to have a position that comes from oppressing others and even fewer would want to live in a world where most of the people around them are suffering oppression.

———

The reason for this last exercise was to highlight how warped a society can become when political power is not fairly distributed. The same case has already begun to exist for our young families due to demographic and societal factors, and chances are that it will get worse if we do not begin now to lead a change.

CHAPTER 5

How to Make the Change Happen

———

THE PROXY VOTE HAS THE potential to broadly change our nation, economy and culture. The greatest change would come through the improvement of the lives of children and their families, renewing the nation's promise by shifting the power to support young people of the nation in their formative years. This simple change is centrally important to reestablishing the core competitive advantage of democracy – allowing citizens to decide for themselves how the government can help to maximize their own potential and their pursuit of happiness. Democracy operates like an efficient and open free market, where the decisions of each individual can optimize the whole, rather than turning to an expert, monarch, wise man, central bureaucrat, or aristocrat to decide what's best. But to achieve that, each citizen must participate, and we must properly manage the outside influences, like big money and influential organizations which are not representative.

When children are directly represented, the bipartisan intentions of the aspiration of "No Child Left Behind" can be made a reality in education, as the most accessible example, and also in many other areas. The proxy vote would apply the power to support the promise of "We the People" bringing another important group into inclusion in a representative government and may lead other democracies towards the renewal of their struggling systems. Imagine the impact on the children raised in that generation and the ones to follow.

Doing nothing is also a choice. There are already changes underway, many accelerating, which combine to threaten all of us with a dystopian outcome beyond the primary effects of the often highlighted issues of an aging population. Newton's law, also known as the "law of inertia", tells us that objects will keep on doing what they're doing, unless some force acts upon them. We know that it applies to human nature as well. Either we overcome the inertia that leads us to do nothing, or we go with the inertia of the current direction of our society which offers increasing challenges for the coming generation. Between the noise of our conflicted society and the natural inertia, the barriers to gaining focus on these issues are extremely high.

Beyond simple inertia, the attempt to make this change will be vehemently opposed by enormous forces. There are many categories of special interests which will conclude that this change would not be to their advantage and will therefore commit resources to prevent any action. Since the change is unprecedented, it will be easy to challenge the fairness and logic of providing a proxy for minor citizens; in our social media world it is certain to be framed comically or viciously.

This chapter begins to outline how the change to the proxy would be made. It first reviews the process issues, suggesting some options for who would control the proxy vote and how the process of exercising the proxy might proceed. This discussion is at the surface level since there are many ways to execute this, and the choices between the alternatives can be decided later. The important point is that it's possible to establish fair and relatively simple rules, and the process issues can be overcome easily enough, relative to the importance of including the 25% of the population that are minors.

How to change

1) Rules and logistics for executing the proxy
2) How to overcome the opposition and the inertia
   * The arguments against will be the same as in the past
   * Advocates and opponents
   * The process of winning the vote – potential path and timing

How to change – rules and process for executing the proxy
Possible rules for assigning and using the proxy:

1) The proxy can be created at the same time as other government documents, e.g. the birth certificate or social security card.
2) The proxy for each child would be assigned to the parents or guardian with legal custody and shared for shared custody situations. It could only be transferred with a legal change of custody. For example:
   * A two-parent family - each parent would have one half of a proxy vote for the child, along with their own normal vote.
   * A single parent with sole custody and 3 children would have the 3 proxy votes along with their own normal vote.
   * Guardians with custody, for example grandparents or relatives or non-relatives with custody, would have the same proxy vote. There are other variations which could be more complex but each one could be resolved.
3) Security around the assignment, movement and verification of the proxy will be needed. This should be simple enough with existing technology but will require the political will to put this in place.
4) Similarly, tracking proxy assignment and voter identification would need to be instituted. These should not be a barrier relative to the importance and impact of the vote but will again require the political will to overcome the opponents.
5) Voter fraud laws may need to be strengthened to prevent abuse of proxy voting by people not directly connected to the minor.

It should not be necessary to say that these will need to be established in a way that does not suppress the vote. Laws and a system to ensure that everyone has access to voter identification will be needed to ensure that no voters are excluded, especially the poor, the elderly, disabled or minority voters.

How to change – overcoming opposition and inertia.
The arguments against the proxy will be similar to those used to exclude other groups:

Anticipated Arguments Against a Proxy Vote	
Argument	Response
The interests of minors are already well represented by the votes of others – their parents and other adults.	This same argument, that their interests are already represented was used against expanding the franchise to include women. The argument was that fathers and husbands would consider the requirements of women in their decisions. "I do not believe the state of Georgia has sunk so low that her good men cannot legislate for women." Mildred Rutherford, president of the Georgia United Daughters of the Confederacy.[91] (Wheeler, 1993) – For African Americans, and Asian Americans the franchise has varied by state and through the first 180 years of the nation's history with some states protecting voting rights from the beginning, and no states allowing voting rights for slaves. Dred Scott reinforced these ideas by stating that former slaves could not have the rights of citizens. Many believed that the representation of citizens who had greater knowledge, wealth, and power was sufficient to make the best decisions for government. It is absurd to believe that the even the most enlightened citizens, even deeply moral and ethical people who believed in equality, could properly represent others, in this case, wealthier white males representing all women and male African-Americans, Asian-Americans and other excluded groups.

They are not contributing to society so should not have a voice	This argument suggests that right to vote comes with an obligation of a certain contribution to the economy or to society. It is not an argument which is consistent with the concept of democracy in the U.S. with one person receiving one vote. Here are some simple conflicts with the logic of using contribution as a filter:
	
	   — Should paying taxes during an election year be a requirement to maintain citizenship and voting rights?
	   — Should there be a net assets threshold?
	   — Does one have to be a current member in the military or a veteran? Contributed community service?
	   — Should the higher contributors receive more votes?
	
	Thresholds of wealth, power, knowledge, religion, poll taxes, etc. have been used to separate and assign the vote to subgroups of citizens in the past. To remain consistent with a true democracy, an Authentic Democracy, all of these should have no footing.

This will overweight the political power of young families with children	Since it represents one vote for each citizen, it is fair by the definition of true democratic representation. The parents with the proxy will not just be concerned about their children, but will also have an interest in all of their own needs and those of the rest of the population e.g. the economy, society, concern for their own parents and other older Americans, etc. There is no reason to expect an unfair rebalancing. But one should expect a fair and equitable rebalancing.

Parents cannot be trusted to vote the interests of their children.	– In the same way that we vote for a representative government which represents adult voters, parents are in the best position to vote to represent their children.
	– Compared to the full responsibility that the parent has over a child's future, the representation through the proxy is relatively small.
	– There is mixed quality in decision-making in the general population, which will also be the case with parents' use of the proxy. We have that through any democratic voting process, and it is the cost of providing free market choice rather than being run by an oligarchy or bureaucracy.
	– Nothing about this proposal necessarily creates better informed citizens, but as with all democracies, we must have enough respect for our fellow adult Americans to believe that they will seek to act in the best interest of their families and their nation. That respect is essential for our democracy and we must overcome the vitriolic politics of our time to remember this if we want to create a better world.

How to change – how to overcome the opposition and inertia
Advocates and opponents

Most politicians of the two leading parties will not champion this change and many may actively oppose it if it begins to gain traction. The change may threaten the embedded incumbents and the broader group that has influence and power. Since it is uncertain how the proxy votes would shift power, it may be viewed as a threat to the broad political establishment. The new votes may create required change in policy positions or affect who is chosen as a representative. Even though the change may not be immediate, it will create some uncertainty for incumbents until a new normal is established. The risk of becoming a champion of such a large change is high, since this idea can easily be made to sound unserious or even comical and may be easy to ridicule, so any politician supporting it too early may risk making a career limiting move; one which future opponents may use in future election cycles. Although successful implementation of the change would affect every future vote, there is no constituency demanding this, so there is not sufficient energy to create movement, and certainly not enough to overcome the inevitable resistance. There are enough special interest groups and issues for representatives to contend with, so only a representative who deeply believed in this could take the risk. Finally, at the party level, the results of the change are difficult to predict, so it is very difficult to assess which party should want to advocate for it and which would resist.

The Democratic Party should be big supporters, since the representatives of minors may align with the Democratic Party's stated priorities – support for social programs, more supportive of culture change, and more willing to support higher taxes. The change might accelerate the shift in voting demographics to a higher proportion of diverse groups and groups with more diverse outlooks. However, the stereotypes of parties and the beliefs of citizens may not be relied upon as accurate and are not easily known. The family age group may be more concerned about the growth of the deficit and the burden it places on future generations. That priority could place additional pressure on reducing government spending growth. It may encourage politicians to highlight plans to directly impact the size of government and have a negative impact on negotiations with government unions at the Federal, State, and Local level, all which align with the Democratic Party. The Democratic Party is also more aligned with the Entertainment and News Media, leading the left side of the culture wars. Those interest groups may be concerned that the potential shift of power towards families may constrain or modify their priorities.

Democrats may also be concerned about any reduction of the power of the academy, which they recognize as a secure ideological base. The threat of changes to the methods of financial aid or the tax protected status of the academy may be deemed unacceptable and may be defended on the grounds that it would impact low income citizens. Collectively there is much for the Democratic Party to resist.

In the same way, the Republican Party also has reason to be big supporters, many of them the near opposite of the Democratic Party's concerns. Although the family vote will support government programs, their concerns about limiting the growth in the Federal Debt may keep government program growth in check, but that may include some of the Republican Party's favored spending areas. The Republican Party may also be aware that married citizens tend to vote Republican at higher levels, though with reductions in the numbers of the young married, and with the proportion of children born and raised in married households decreasing, this may not help them. On the other hand, Republican's rely on a larger proportion of votes of older Americans who may see the change as a threat to pensions, Medicare, and Social Security. Others may fear that it will drive more accelerated social change, with an increase in the voting weight of younger citizens who view the world differently. They may also be concerned about changes to drug or crime policies, making them more lenient or costly. Collectively, there is much for the Republican Party to resist. However, they may view the longer term impact on education as a way to ensure growth of the economy and the way to ensure that the United States retains leadership in technology and defense.

How the additional votes from the proxy will swing the nation's politics is difficult to accurately predict in advance of full implementation. It is not possible to use historic polling or survey data, to achieve a reasonably accurate simulation for how past elections might have been different with the additional proxy votes. Historic data would also lack an accurate consideration of how politicians would modify platforms and messaging to influence the additional votes. (Of course, the fact that they would modify platforms is exactly why the proxy should be created!). Therefore, neither party would have sufficient information to predict the outcome, so it could be in the interest of the established politicians in both dominant parties to maintain the status quo until they are forced to make a change.

The strongest supporters will be citizens who choose to support the idea because they deeply believe in the value of democracy to transform the world, and who note that there are several areas like those outlined above where we are failing the next generation because the government is not properly recognizing these citizens as constituents and not hearing their voices. Since most parents have limited free time, it will require many of those beyond child-rearing stage, and before child rearing stage, and perhaps some who have chosen to remain child-free, to actively support this because of the belief that every citizen should be represented.

How to change – how to overcome the opposition and inertia. The process of winning the vote – potential plan
The Systematic Approach
There is no single and certain path to making this change happen, but the most obvious way to begin is the same as for any movement: building a core team of supporters, expanding by building awareness, distributing initiatives regionally to establish some successes, managing the opposition, building momentum and adjusting from there. Since this is not even out of the starting blocks, it isn't worth diving deeper beyond the listing of items shown below.

Build a team and align the natural supporters

* Attract support from citizens who are natural supporters
  o Parents of minors
  o Young adults not yet parents
  o Grandparents
  o Minors

  o Aligning with other initiatives to support minors
- Child Welfare Groups
- Education organizations
- Foundations
- Philanthropists
- Corporations

Launch efforts to build awareness and support
- Web presence
- Targeted email campaign
- News media and press
- Convince pollsters to begin collecting and publishing data in their polls

Establish a leader in the most promising states and expand to each of 50 states; support their independent initiatives.

Prepare for the opposition.

Achieve critical mass in selected local and state areas to win establishing the proxy.

Assess ability to move more quickly towards national momentum.

Adjust from there.

CHAPTER 6

Final Thoughts

———

The defense of minors is a noble cause. The image that I'd like to leave you with: Think of a time when you were in a situation of a large crowd in a tight area – a subway, a concert, a sporting event, an airport, etc. In these situations, the crowd of otherwise very good and smart people, can sometimes quickly turn into a mob, moving or behaving without considering others, willing to push or even trample a fellow human in a way that none of the individuals would ever intend to do under normal circumstances. It may take some catalyst to set them off, or it may just build spontaneously, but they will sometimes lose control. Some of the people are selfish or scared, and they will do whatever it takes to get what they want. That behavior can become contagious. Then herd behavior takes over. Now, think of young children in that crowd. They are helpless in this situation and easily trampled. The parents try to cordon them off or find a corner, but the size of the crowd is daunting. That is where we are today. The image that I'd like to leave you with is this - we must form a cordon around those children. As many of us as are willing and courageous enough to hold the line against the crowd. It doesn't matter who the children are or who we are, the rest of the crowd will unwittingly trample them until enough of us commit to forming a barrier around them to protect their lives and future.

* By now, the connection of the lead page stating the Old Greek proverb will be obvious "A society grows great when old men plant trees whose shade they know they will never sit in." It is both true and fitting. It highlights that the investment in planting and cultivating a tree is a long term investment in the future, and that a great society is created when citizens are willing to make a personal contribution to others by investing in that future.

Thank you for reading this!

How you can Help

———

CHAPTER SEVEN: A PLAN FOR immediate next steps

- Visit the website or Facebook: *in process so please Google search for Authentic Democracy*
- Support the concept by mentioning "Authentic Democracy" or the "Proxy Vote for Children" in conversation, blog, Facebook, etc.
- Recommend this book to someone

APPENDIX A: THE GROWING CHALLENGE OF POWERFUL ORGANIZATIONS

––––

THERE ARE SEVERAL CATEGORIES OF powerful organizations which compete to influence government policy and direction. They do so through many means, including influencing citizens on the choice of representatives, influencing the representatives directly, to influencing the many government agencies. Among the most powerful organizations are corporations, public sector unions, journalist media, many single issue ideology groups, higher education, entertainment media, and transnational organizations.

Corporations

Large corporations represent the largest portion of the economy in the United States and their concentrated power continues to increase. There are no direct measures of their relative contribution to the overall economy, but comparing indirect measures confirms their relative growth and impact on the economy. Comparing Fortune 500 revenue to nominal GDP shows that the ratio has increased from 58 percent of GDP in 1994 to 73 percent in 2013.[92] (Flowers, 2015)

The legal and organizational framework of the corporation has helped to move the entire world to greater prosperity, lower poverty, and innovation across industries, technologies, and the sciences. Corporations provide a legal entity to allow for collective investment with limited liability. Although they existed prior to the 20th century, the laws began to change in the early 20th century to enable the growth of the corporation in the United States. However, the level of power that these organizations now exercise was never envisioned during the nation's founding and our democracy continues to wrestle with developing the proper rules and limits on corporate behavior. There are a broad range of issues from corporate laws to corporate taxation, to regulatory constraints, to limits on competitive behavior, and more recently, emerging issues from social media surrounding privacy, censorship and political activity.

Corporations have a frequent need to influence the decisions of government officials since the results of government action have high impact on corporate performance. There are some objectives which are shared across corporations like reducing corporate taxes, but most of the issues are specific to the industry sector. For example, the finance and insurance industries are each affected by extensive regulations and therefore have high expenditures towards influencing government actions. While they prefer the lower costs that come with less regulations, the large companies in these sectors benefit from the barrier to entry created by these regulations which smaller competitors cannot afford to meet. Regulations to control their behavior often lead to the reverse of what government regulators may intend, concentrating the power among fewer financial firms. These companies can sometimes posture to appear to be virtuous in supporting stiff regulations, when in fact it can be a self-serving stance protecting their business from competition, allowing for higher profit at the expense of the consumer.

Healthcare related industries are always under a regulatory regime and have a similar mixed perspective on government regulations. In more recent years established healthcare companies have become increasingly focused on influencing government actions as a strategic imperative. The electronics and communications industries operate under substantial government regulatory and legal restrictions and seek to influence domestic policy, and work within a global supply network and global customer base, so seek government support for those efforts. The many other large corporate sectors including especially construction, energy and natural resources, automobiles, other transportation, defense, and agriculture, all have their own set of issues which they must seek to influence. The level of union concentration within an industry can increase the need to influence government and to indirectly help to manage union relationships.

Collectively, the need to influence regulatory and congressional decisions results in the need for large businesses and industries to maintain some influence over the government. That need for influence feeds most of the lobbying industry, internal corporate lobbyists, internal regulatory legal staff, and many corporate law firms. Government representatives benefit from the vying for power among these organizations, and the individual power of each representative increases in proportion to the decision making authority they have over the financial and regulatory priorities of the organizations. Government representatives on the right committees have more power than government representatives not on those committees, and growing the government's power in the area where the government representative already has power, gives them even more power and influence.

While many of the objectives of these corporate actions do not conflict directly with the concerns of young families, their objectives and efforts minimally result in taking mindshare to move the corporate issues up in the priority stack. They also sometimes do directly conflict with the obvious preferences and needs of the young family, and there are many examples where our representatives have failed to act in the best interest of families with minors.

Two of the most widely known examples come from the tobacco and entertainment industries. The tobacco industry has not been good for the U.S. citizens, nor to world citizens. Tobacco was an important part of the U.S. economy since the original colonies. It was once among the most highly respected industries, but the planned addiction of millions by tobacco firms is now known to have resulted in a very high number of premature deaths. The CDC estimates that one in five deaths in the

U.S. in 2016 was tobacco related – which is fully 480,000 deaths in one year.[93] (Prevention) (Full disclosure - the writer's father's death in 2014 was premature due to tobacco use). Life expectancy for smokers is fully 10 years shorter than life expectancy for non-smokers.

By the mid 1940's to early 1950's, there was a preponderance of evidence indicating that smoking was causing an epidemic of lung cancer. As a result of litigation won against the tobacco industry, we now know that Phillip Morris, now Altria, and other tobacco companies were aware of the dangers of tobacco products and the addictiveness of nicotine. The industry actively worked to suppress that information from reaching the public and continued to deny the link to carcinogens, though their documents clearly indicated that they had better knowledge.[94] (Proctor, 2013) They actively lobbied their government contacts, fought regulation and were marketing broadly to the population, directly and through advertising and more subtly through placement in TV and movies. As clever marketers, they were targeting the under 18 as the most fertile ground for new customers. All of the tobacco companies' efforts were in clear conflict with the objectives of young families, but that industry's successful legal and regulatory efforts allowed them to continue marketing efforts towards new consumers, especially minors, well after there was sufficient knowledge of the health risks.

A similar example comes from the movie and entertainment industries where parents have long been concerned about the violence level that is regularly presented to minors. Following the tragic 13 deaths at Columbine, Colorado in 1999, President Clinton asked the Federal Trade Commission to investigate the movie, music, and computer and video game industries, to answer two key questions: "Do the industries promote products they themselves acknowledge warrant parental caution in venues where children make up a substantial percentage of the audience? And are these advertisements intended to attract children and teenagers?"[95] (FTC, 2000) The answer to both questions was a clear yes for all three industry sectors – movie, music, and computer and video gaming. Working with industry documents, the FTC determined that, despite the fact that their own rating systems found the material appropriate only for adults, these industries practiced "pervasive and aggressive marketing of violent movies, music, and electronic games to children".

There is no evidence that any effective action has been taken since that time. In fact, the Motion Picture Association of America, the MPAA, has a website MPAA.org which has a section dedicated to "Issues and Positions" and lists among several major topics "Inclusion and Outreach" and "Preserving Free Speech" but nothing related to children or violence. They also post an extensive number of research reports, but nothing could be found at the time this was researched regarding children or violence. However, the facts continue to accumulate that this is a concern for parents, and that concern is well justified. To quote the American Academy of Pediatrics News *"The strength of the association between media violence and aggressive behavior found in meta-analyses is greater than the association between calcium intake and bone mass, lead ingestion and lower IQ, and condom nonuse and sexually acquired HIV infection, and is nearly as strong as the association between cigarette smoking and lung cancer—associations that clinicians accept and on which preventive medicine is based without question."*[96] (Pediatrics, 2009).[97] (Craig A. Anderson, 2003),[98] (L. Rowell Huesmann, 2003),[99] (Hausmann, 2007) [97] *"In addition to modeling violent behavior, entertainment media inflate the prevalence of violence in the world, cultivating in viewers the "mean-world" syndrome, a perception of the world as a dangerous place."*[100] (Brad J. Bushman & L. Rowell Huesmann, 2006)

This is another commonly known example of a situation where there is no noticeable government action because the concerns of powerful large organizations, in this case the corporate sector, outweigh any voting power of the young family. There is not sufficient political requirement or potential for a successful campaign for families to band together to rival the economic and public relations engine of the entertainment industry. Any parent group which attempts to challenge the entertainment industry will either be ignored by the controlling interests in the media, or characterized as religious fanatics or Luddites, to ensure that the group is quickly dismissed and not given supporting publicity.

Public Sector Employees and Unions The group of employees working in the public sector is a powerful force in U.S. politics. The public sector includes employees at the federal, state and local level totaling a full 22.3 Million employees by May 2017, or 18% of the total of all employment in the private sector. The 1.4 M military personnel are not included in the public sector numbers, though the Department of Defense personnel is included.

The public services provided by these employees are essential to young families, and many of the government functions are essential to every citizen. The largest group of public service employees is in education, most at the state and local level, with 10.4 Million employees representing 46.6 % of all federal, state, and local government employees. That is equal to approximately 7 times the size of all combined branches of all U.S. military personnel. The next largest group is in law enforcement and the judiciary, with approximately 2.3 Million or 10.3% between officers, judicial and correctional facility employees, followed by hospitals with 1.1 Million and fire protection at 0.4 Million. Other major public sector groups work in the U.S. Postal Service, highways, health, public welfare, parks and recreation, libraries, natural resources, water, sewers, and waste management.

The power of the public sector employee group and their unions is a relatively new phenomenon in the United States, though most citizens are not aware of this fact. Over time it has become the new normal. The original unions were formed by private sector employees to address important workers issues in the early part of the 20th century. During the union movement's early development, Franklin Delano Roosevelt, long a champion of union workers rights openly articulated resistance to expanding the power of union bargaining into the public sector. "Meticulous attention should be paid to the special relations and obligations of public servants to the public itself and to the Government," he cautioned. "The process of collective bargaining, as usually under-stood, cannot be transplanted into the public service."[101] (Schmitt, 2014) During the 1950's, public sector unions began to grow rapidly, and at the same time government grew faster than the private sector. In the late 1950's and early 1960's, legislation expanded the power of public sector unions with two key executive orders – the first from Mayor Robert Wagner Jr. in New York City in 1958 for city employees and then in 1962 by President John Kennedy, allowing the right to bargain collectively for federal employees.

Coinciding with this expansion of public sector union rights was an increase in the size of the public sector relative to the private sector. From 1950 to 1975, the non-farm private sector increased 73% in size, while the federal, state and local government sector increased by a factor of 145%, from 6.0M to 14.7M. In absolute terms, that is from 13.5% of the size of the non-farm private sector to 18%. (In 1900 it was 4%). During that same period, the state and local government portion excluding federal, tripled, growing from 4 to 12 million. From 1950 to now, the U.S. population has increased from 152M to 325M, or 113 percent increase, while the size of the government employment has increased from 6.0 to 22.3 Million or a 271 percent increase.[102] (Tucker, 1981)

As a result of this growth, public sector employees now comprise a large portion of the voting public and can rally members as a group to promote the issues which they deem important. The employees are highly organized through their unions, with fully 34.4 % of public sector employees signing as union members, a rate more than 5 times that of the private sector rate of 6.4%. The public sector union leadership understands the power of political activity and wield that power very effectively. Reaching well beyond organizing their members, they use union finances to fund important elections, use disruptive strikes and protests to sway public opinion, and concentrate national level power on the local and state elections that are most important to them. They align with the Democratic Party, but are able to influence both major parties through the high level of power that they wield. They have proven highly effective at strategically applying power and resources where needed to protect their area of influence.

The power of public sector employees as a group and their unions as organizations is highly relevant to the consideration of the proxy vote. Their concentrated power has the impact of prioritizing union and public sector employees' issues above the general population of citizens who they are employed to serve. Under the current system, the public sector personnel and unions have disproportionate impact compared to the average group of citizens and by tightly aligning their power, can overwhelm the votes of the parents and guardians of minor children. Their sources of power derive from four core areas – 1) Concentration and homogeneity of votes of their large population of members who can be guided by the union leadership towards preferred candidates and referendums; 2) Application of national power to local issues when an issue is important to their strategy; 3) Application of insider knowledge as government workers to influence outcomes vs. the general citizen group; 4) Alignment and extensive influence with one of the two major political parties, ensuring advocacy in most contentious issues.

The first of these is the concentration of votes through their large group of members to support the issues that they deem important. Public sector personnel directly command large blocks of votes compared to the rest of the citizen population. Since the general population splits fairly evenly between the two major parties, any group which can be aligned to be nearly homogeneous in their voting can command high influence to sway an election. Since members receive guidance from the union on how to vote, they wield tremendous power. Group discipline creates strategic voting power.

The second is that the union has the ability to provide concentrated financial support to their chosen party and issue, bringing national scale and power to smaller local contests. They mobilize union members, hire paid protesters, apply financial resources, and have a successful track record of demonstrated ability to overcome challenges to their power. As national organizations, their power can overcome local challenges to their hegemony on issues important to them, completely overwhelming a fair and open democracy at the local level and effectively cheating what is intended in a democratic system. Their effectiveness frightens off future challenges, since only the naïve would not realize the potential firestorm that can result from a challenge.

The third area of power is from the continuity, knowledge and personal priority of its members on issues that affect their daily work lives as employees. Contrast that to a private citizen who experiences the service and cost as a consumer. One only partially hypothetical example - a parent with a child in a failing school in California may decide to become involved to attempt to improve the situation, and along with other parents attempt to use the California Parent Empower Act to close or convert a poorly performing school campus. They would inevitably tread in areas where the union, teachers, administrators and a biased school board would prefer not challenged. That parent would have far fewer years of involvement, continuity, and relationships than the professional teachers, union members and the school board (invariably partly composed of union or former union members.) The parents have little of the expertise or free time, and the institutions will fight, while being paid for their efforts. The weight is all on the side of the institutions, leaving citizens relatively powerless in addressing something that free citizens should control. It is not quite the deep state that some citizens fear but approaches that in the result.

The fourth area of power comes from the strategic and national level alignment that most public sector unions have with a single political party – the Democratic Party (though this may not be so with the police union). That cooperative relationship can guarantee that there is always one party ensuring that the interests of the union will be considered first. One of the best examples of that level of power comes from Senator Corey Booker of New Jersey, one of the most promising political leaders in the United States. As mayor of Newark, he was a staunch advocate for charter schools and school choice. This was consistent with his constituents needs, with the polling of Newark parents show-ing that 71% supporting the expansion of the charter schools. He held to his position when strongly opposed by the Newark Teachers Union in his 2010 reelection campaign, prioritizing the needs of children and their families. However, now serving at the national level as Senator Booker, he voted against the Senate confirmation vote for Secretary of Education Betsy DeVos, who was arguably the most accomplished advocate for charter schools. He explained that he was not satisfied with her responses to congressional questions, but of course answers to congressional questions are nothing compared to the evidence of a lifetime of achievements and actions from a known advocate of improv-ing schools and supporting alternatives choices that improve outcomes. This was not hypocrisy on Senator Booker's part, but rather a pragmatic understanding of national politics and power in the current political environment.

This example is the archetype of the dangerous distortion to democ-racy that occurs through the lack of minor's representation. In this case, the teachers who are members of the teachers' unions are individ-ually highly concerned with the needs of minors, and most presumably believe that they act and vote consistent with those priorities. However, the organization of a union and its leadership is directed to very specific objectives of maintaining maximum employment, wages, and benefits and continuing to maintain and expand influence. Any attempt by par-ents to overcome the union's objectives, like closing underperforming schools or expanding charter schools challenges their primary objec-tives. (They will strongly disagree, but the facts are obvious. The same as for the leaders of any organization, union leadership is expected to grow and improve the financial position of its members.) Corey Booker was willing to risk his early career to improve children's public educa-tion, but as he moved from local to national politics, he had to conform to the requirements of the party, and therefore the union.

If minors had a proxy vote, the results should be very favorable for most teachers, though not for all teachers. The proxy votes will raise society's prioritization of education, and therefore will more highly value and compensate effective teachers. As in private industry, the drive to improve performance will raise wages and the natural competition to recruit, develop, and retain effective teachers will help establish a broader ecosystem of support to make those teachers even more effective. The supporting functions, of education technology and physical infrastructure of schools would also improve. Poor performing and problem administrators and teachers would not do so well, and could not be protected, though as with private industry, it would be naïve to think that these are quickly and easily identified and resolved. Nor should we be misled to believe that the nation's education issues are simply a financial issue or rest on poor performing teachers. It is a more complex issue with broad societal factors. Nevertheless, a large portion of the solution may be on different terms than the union leadership will currently accept, and their defense of low performing or problem teachers may leave them fighting any new initiatives. Over time, the union leadership will recognize the new reality and adapt, so the proxy vote should become a win-win-win for students, teachers and the unions. (Tuttle, 2017)[103]

The growth in power and size of public sector unions is relatively recent and the nation faces some risks in that they might learn to further leverage their power disproportionate to the power of the average citizen. Their ability to use funds and internal influence to determine the representatives who then negotiate their compensation and benefits is unheard of in the private sector. The analogy in the private sector would be to allow the employees to periodically determine who will be the manager or CEO, with the CEO or manager then having the authority to determine employee compensation and benefit levels, with no measure of profit to limit bad behavior. It would be a generous place with easy work rules, disproportionately high job security, compensation, and other benefits well above market rates. In the private sector, this would create a business that would eventually fail. That disproportionate power is not a new thought or finding, it is common knowledge, and well understood by union leadership. This quote comes from as far back as 1975, from a union leader, Victor Gotbaum, the leader of Council 37 of AFSCME in New York City, stating in 1975, "We have the ability, in a sense, to elect our own boss." They are more subtle now and do not broadcast this, but the case is the same and it is a direct challenge to the U.S. democratic representation. It is not a good system!

As with other major power groups, the mindshare that is applied to the interests and needs of this powerful group has the effect of subordinating the interests of young families, shifting the focus of representatives away from the issues of the young family. Beyond mindshare, the unions have cleverly determined that negotiating longer term benefits, like larger pensions and easy pension rules, is easier to negotiate with government representatives than current wages which are more visible. This shifts cost to debts that are off the books, but that minors will need to pay in the future. The results are large unfunded pension obligations placed upon the young families, and effectively transferred to the minors. Those longer term government workers benefits have created large unfunded pension liabilities in many states – discussed in chapter 2. All adding costs to future generations of Americans.

Journalist Media
Americans consume a vast amount of news each day from many different sources and through a variety of media. The media include published newspapers, magazines, local and network broadcast TV, cable TV, streaming video, radio, podcast, and internet. The media industry has been growing and migrating the types of delivery format method for some time, initially from print, then adding radio and TV, cable, then internet and now streaming. There has been a recent steady decline in print, with a reduction in the number of print newspapers and lower advertising revenue, with weekday circulation falling 7% between 2010 and 2015 and ad revenue dropping over 30% in that time. In 2017, weekday print newspaper circulation dropped 11% to 31 million, approximately half of circulation in 1980.[104] (Pew

Research Center: Journalism and Media) The decline has occurred with the rise of others, particularly with cable and network TV growing, along with internet and streaming, along with a sharp increase in digital advertising.

Most Americans place a high value on being up to date on current information. The categories of information, and what people chose to follow is driven by individual preference and includes U.S. economy, U.S. politics, local news, world events, weather, sports, new innovations, entertainment news, gossip, etc. The media organizations choose what to provide and their editorial posture is based on many factors including their brand focus, advertiser concerns, information from others in the industry, etc. There is some evidence that media personnel monitor each other's reports and messages closely and act unintentionally as a giant echo chamber, sometimes magnifying issues that seem to resonate with each other and their target groups. For some time, the Republican Party has been claiming a national media bias towards positioning the Democratic Party favorably. There is no scholarly research to prove this, although a survey of journalists by the Indiana University School of Journalism[105] (Weaver, 2014) indicates a moderate slant in media personnel's personal political alignment, with 28% declaring Democratic versus 7% Republicans, with 50% declaring Independent and the remaining 15% other. These results can be assessed as a modest slant of 21 %, or it can be assessed as a 4 to 1 ratio or discounted as quite uncertain since so many are not fully indicating an affiliation.

There are two primary problems in the effect on young families from the media. The first is one of crowding the mindshare which should be applied to real issues, as the media creates noise that is wrapped as news. They seek the interesting and immediate and knowingly sensationalize. As a result, they crowd out the very real and important issues that should be on the minds of citizens. The second is that the media as any group of professionals has biases, and it imposes its views of what is important, magnified in an echo chamber and through a megaphone. They directly move the general public's views through their role, determining which topics will be perceived as important, and then apply a sense of immediacy and importance to a select issue.

The first affect, taking mindshare, simply changes the attention of individuals to, for the extreme trivial example, some celebrity's fashion choices or how cute a koala bear is, a recent birth at the zoo, or a verbal stumble by a politician, instead of maintaining focus on very real longer term important issues that would more directly affect citizens. The second occurs when media coverage directly influences which issues are highlighted and the slant used to view the political position of many important tradeoffs throughout the country and world. The categories that are chosen will by default map well to what is important to the journalists and advertisers, as opposed to the average citizen.

Since children would not necessarily be in that target market of these, and since more disposable income is important to advertisers interested in consumption, it is natural that the priorities are not the same as what they would be for young families. In addition, the journalists themselves are very different than the young family member so would naturally have different concerns. The median age of journalists has been rising at a steady pace since 1982 at 32 years, in the range of child rearing, to 36 in 1992, 41 in 2002, and 47 in 2013. On average, journalists are now at a later age than most families with minors. It is quickly becoming a much older group.

Single Issue Ideology Groups
There are many single issue ideology groups which compete for the attention of the public and will continue to attract a high level of attention relative to the issues that truly effect the 75M minors and their families. They include groups taking opposite sides on many political issues, including gun control groups vs. gun rights groups, pro-choice groups and pro-life groups, climate change and environmental groups vs. industries which use or produce carbon based fuels, and many movements like LGBT rights groups, affirmative action groups, the Black

Lives Matter movement, etc. Many of these groups are now funded by foundations, very wealthy citizens or political action committees. Most of these are movements that address some real needs and reasonable views, however, as more concentrated money flows into these organizations, it becomes less clear if the groups are championing the real priorities of citizens, or are the results of citizens who are paid members of organizations used to champion the excess of select wealthy individuals or extremist groups. The end result of some of this is similar to the days when the aristocracy or the king's court was powerful and sought to determine the direction of a nation through intrigue and clever influence.

The issues of these single interest groups are highly important to their supporters and most seek to build membership rolls with people who view and prioritize these issues as the most central to building a better world. Most have some core involvement in the culture wars. However, although a few of the issues affect the future rights and freedoms of children and young families, overall they do not represent any balance of the issues that families would necessarily chose as priorities. The single issue interest groups wield tremendous power on both sides of the aisle in determining the battleground issues. By controlling the national discussion without any representation of a quarter of the population, the priorities and conclusions on these issues are inevitably not representative.

Higher education establishment
Colleges and Universities have played a part in the national political debate for some time, and their reach and power have continued to increase substantially in recent years. That growth is partly due to immense growth in the number if students attending and graduating college both in absolute numbers and as percentage of the population, and due to the increase in costs related to the higher education of each individual student. It was not long ago that only a small portion of the population received a college degree – in 1940 less than 5% of the

population over 25 had earned a degree; by 2009 it had increased by a factor of 5 to 30%. At the same time, university tuition has substantially outpaced inflation, as discussed earlier, increasing their portion of the economy. Another part of their growth in power and reach is related to the media's need to turn to the academy as expert commentators and as the source of ideas for interesting stories or supporting comments. Contributing to this growth in power is the wealth and financial security among the more established universities, allowing their faculty to become more militant and politically active.

Not long ago, the political party leanings of universities and faculties were more heterogeneous and not displayed in the way that is now obvious. That change is notable across the full spectrum of university leadership, from the composition of the Board of Trustees, to the university president or provost, to the speakers who are invited to campus or commencement, to those who are given honorary degrees and awards.

The reason this is relevant is that academic professionals often select the issues and create a substantial amount of the messages that become the discussion topics of society and the discourse of policy makers. They educate the thought leaders of tomorrow and promote opinions which they present as fact. They direct the research that is then used as evidence for the answers that they believe are important and correct. While they can sometimes have alignment to the needs of young families, they more often crowd out the voices of young families and capture mindshare in a very different way than the other powerful forces. They can use the patina of intelligence and the branding of diplomas, to exercise influence on topics which are often only peripherally related to their expertise to create a halo over their opinions, to encourage a higher acceptance of their views. This is especially persuasive to the young adult's aged 18-25 who are in their care, in early stages of maturity, but before taking on any real responsibility which would have provided a more informed understanding of the world.

Entertainment Media and Industry

The entertainment industry has an opinion and they are not shy about sharing it at every opportunity through what they create and in how they communicate with the entertainment news media. This is not new and is a normal function of the performing arts. By the very nature of the industry, it attracts people who want to communicate, be noticed, valued, and respected. The problem for minors is that the entertainment media has grown in power as a political force because of the amount of media consumed, the new levels of reach of the many media outlets, and simply because of the growth in their economic power. As a group, they have become arbiters on many issues and frequently show little humility in determining which viewpoints are correct and prescribing what others should believe. They have a powerful amplifier to deliver their preferred messages without fear of challenge by an opposing view. They therefore can exercise excessive power and influence on the culture's values and choices over what is deemed important, despite the fact that few lead lives even remotely similar to their audience. Their power is highly disproportionate to their numbers and is not related to any special skill or insight in areas related to selection of representatives – economics, law, history, politics, world affairs, healthcare, etc. Since they are constantly in the limelight and micro analyzed by the entertainment news media, they have become experts at virtue signaling. They do this in a way that is entertaining, and therefore quite effective, especially when directed to younger minds.

These comments do not suggest a way or good reason to limit the communication of this successful industry. It is the free exercise of their rights and profession and there is not a way to change this that remains consistent with constitutional freedoms. The proxy vote would not change this. These comments are only meant to highlight that this is another group of organizations that drive national priorities with disproportionate power and distinctly different outlooks and priorities from the general U.S. population. Their messages can overwhelm or drown out the voices of the needs of the young families. The proxy would help to move some power and greater focus on the needs of the young family group, helping them to keep the focus on their known needs and vote towards achieving their own goals.

Transnational Organizations and other Nations

Many nations and multinational organizations seek to influence the choices and beliefs of the voting population, of government representatives, and of the government agencies. The list is long and broad and include the governments of most large nations, including allies and competitors, like the United Kingdom, Germany, Canada, France, Mexico, Japan, Israel, Saudi Arabia, South Korea, Egypt, Turkey, China, and Russia, among others. Each interacts at various levels and seeks different levels of attention. Naturally they attempt to determine our national direction and seek to influence voters, advocate for issues directly or through advocacy groups, and sometimes discreetly, improperly, or illegally.

As a leading global power economically and militarily, the U.S. is a member of many organizations, and is under the influence of those organizations and fellow member states. These include the large number multinational organizations like the United Nations, European Union, World Bank, NATO, World Trade Organization, International Monetary Fund, World Health Organization, etc. and many, many nongovernmental organizations.

Citizens of other nations and other multinational organizations try to influence U.S. decisions. That should not be surprising to anyone, just as U.S. citizens and organizations seek to influence the decision of other nations through membership in multinational organizations. The point for this discussion is that these organizations and nations are another force that draw power and priority from the issues of minors. Most of these countries and organizations do not have much interest in the needs and concerns of U.S. citizens who are minors, and their focus will be on other issues. Representation of minors does not conflict with the activities of these organizations, but that representation will more properly balance the focus of representatives and government on the issues of minor citizens when they must compete for priority with foreign organizations.

———

None of this discussion suggests that we create additional constraints upon free speech, nor upon the ability of organizations to actively lobby representatives to best achieve their objectives. Instituting any constraints would bring a new set of problems. This only seeks to highlight that the power of large organizations and industry sectors further marginalize the influence of minors and their families. The nation must restore a better balance by implementing a proxy vote for minors.

ENDNOTES

1. Michael Schuyler, *A Short History of Government Taxing and Spending in the United States - Tax Foundation*, 2014; https://taxfoundation.org/short-history-government-taxing-and-spending-united-states/

2. Federal Reserve Bank of Saint Louis, Economic Research, Fertility rate of Total United States; https://fred.stlouisfed.org/series/SPDYNTFRTINUSA

3. "U.S. Households by Size, 1790–2006." Infoplease.© 2000-2017 Sandbox Networks, Inc., publishing as Infoplease.9 Jul. 2017 https://www.infoplease.com/us/household-and-family-statistics/us-households-size-1790-2006

4. Jonathan Vespa, Jamie M. Lewis, and Rose M. Kreider, America's Families and Living Arrangements: 2012 Population Characteristics; United States Census Bureau, Issued August 2013. https://www.census.gov/prod/2013pubs/p20-570.pdf

5. Bureau of Labor Statistics, American Time Use Survey https://www.bls.gov/news.release/pdf/atus.pdf

6. The 4.3 hours per day of leisure time seems higher than one would expect, but may be inflated by the 25-44 year olds who chose to be childfree bringing the average up to that number.

7. UN Population Division 2017; Ourwordindata.org; https://our-worldindata.org/grapher/historic-and-un-pop-projections-by-age?time=1960..2100&country=USA

8. Mauro, P., Romeu, R., Binder, A., & Zaman, A. (2015). A modern history of fiscal prudence and profligacy. Journal of Monetary Economics, 76, 55-70.

9.   OurworldinData.Org; Government Spending % of GDP, Max Roser, OurWorldinData.org, https://ourworldindata.org/government-spending; Original Source: Mauro, P., Romeu, R., Binder, A., & Zaman, A. (2015). A modern history of fiscal prudence and profligacy. Journal of Monetary Economics, 76, 55-70. Government expenditure estimates correspond to non-interest government expenditures. The authors als0 note: "The database covers an unbalanced panel of 55 countries (24 advanced economies—by present day definition from the IMF's World Economic Outlook classification—and 31 nonadvanced) over 1800–2011. The data consist of government revenue, non-interest government expenditure, and the interest bill (and thus also the overall fiscal balance and the primary balance), as well as gross public debt, all expressed as a share of GDP...About half of the observations for the fiscal variables in our dataset are drawn from various cross-country sources, including the IMF's World Economic Outlook (WEO) and International Financial Statistics (IFS) and the OECD Analytical Database...We hand-collected the other half of the data from country-specific sources, such as official government publications or economic histories that included public finance statistics." IMF data on government expenditure does not include interest paid on debt payments. In order to derive government expenditure with interest paid on debt included, the datasets "government expenditure, percent of GDP" and "interest paid on public debt, percent of GDP" from the IMF database.

10.   Who's Up, Who's Down? View industries with the greatest increases and decreases in lobbying spending by quarter and by year 2019. https://www.opensecrets.org/lobby/incdec.php

11.   Political Parties (Spending 2016), Center for Responsive Politics https://www.opensecrets.org/parties/index.php?cmte=&cycle=2016

12. Feenstra, Robert C., Robert Inklaar and Marcel P. Timmer (2015), "The Next Generation of the Penn World Table" American Economic Review, 105(10), 3150-3182, available for download at www.ggdc.net/pwt

13. Hilbert and Cairo, 2008; Cristopher Freeman et al. As time goes by, 2001. Schumpeter, (1939). Business Cycles: A Theoretical, Hist., & Stat. Analysis of the Capitalist Process.

14. Employment, Skills and Workforce Strategy for the Fourth Industrial Revolution, 2016 World Economic Forum. http://www3.weforum.org/docs/WEF_Future_of_Jobs.pdf

15. U.S. Debt Clock.org; https://www.usdebtclock.org/

16. Just How Much Land Does the Federal Government Own — and Why? Frank Jacobs, July 2010. https://bigthink.com/strange-maps/291-federal-lands-in-the-us

17. Federal Assets Above and Below Ground, Institute For Energy Research, 2013; https://www.instituteforenergyresearch.org/fossil-fuels/coal/federal-assets-above-and-below-ground/

18. The Declining Significance of Age in the United States: Trends in the Well-Being of Children and the Elderly since 1939, Eugene Smolensky, Sheldon Danziger, Peter Gottschalk https://www.irp.wisc.edu/publications/dps/pdfs/dp83987.pdf

19. Poverty Rate by Age, Henry J. Kaiser Family Foundation, 2017. https://www.kff.org/other/state-indicator/poverty-rate-by-age/?currentTimeframe=0&sortModel=%7B%22colId%22:%22Locatio n%22,%22sort%22:%22asc%22%7D

20. Social Security Lifetime Benefits and Taxes, C. Eugene Steuerle, Caleb Quakenbush September 16, 2015, https://www.urban.org/ research/publication/social-security-and-medicare-lifetime-benefits-and-taxes

21. The term Ponzi scheme refers to a different process than a pyramid scheme, though there are similarities. Ponzi schemes often use a similar networking effect as pyramid schemes and depend on bringing in an increasing number of people, but there is usually no underlying business or asset. For example, an investor might give a firm $10K as an investor. The firm gives regular reports that the money has appreciated 15% each year to create excitement a fuel word of mouth growth as well as encourage further investment. The original client moves more money into that portfolio since it appears on paper to be growing so consistently, and tells their friends about the wonderful investment, so more money comes in. This continues, regardless of the real financial markets behavior. Occasionally someone makes a withdrawal, but this can continue as long as there are not too many withdrawals. Behind the gains on paper, there may be no increases in investment value or worse, the firm may just be using the money for their own pleasure and operating expenses. The Madoff investment scandal had many of these characteristics, which prosecutors estimated as a $65 Billion fraud.

22. The 2017 Long-Term Budget Outlook. The Congressional Budget Office, The Congress of the United States. https://www.cbo.gov/ system/files/115th-congress-2017-2018/reports/52480-ltbo.pdf

23. C. Eugene Steuerle and Caleb Quakenbush, Social Security and Medicare Lifetime Benefits and Taxes Urban Institute 2015. Based on earlier work with Stephanie Rennane and Adam Carasso. Table 10. Assumes benefits scheduled in law will be paid. Worker works every year starting at age 22 and retires at age 65.

24.   2017 Annual Report Of The Boards Of Trustees Of The Federal Hospital Insurance And Federal Supplementary Medical Insurance Trust Funds, July 13, 2017, Table II.B1 – Medicare Data for Calendar Year 2016, page 10 https://www.cms.gov/Research-Statistics-Data-and-Systems/Statistics-Trends-and-Reports/ReportsTrustFunds/Downloads/TR2017.pdf

25.   Kaiser Family Foundation/Robert Wood Johnson Foundation/Harvard School of Public Health, *The Public's Health Care Agenda for the 113th Congress* (conducted January 3-9, 2013) https://www.kff.org/health-reform/poll-finding/the-publics-policy-agenda-for-the-113th-congress/

26.   2017 Annual Report Of The Boards Of Trustees Of The Federal Hospital Insurance And Federal Supplementary Medical Insurance Trust Funds, July 13, 2017, Table II.B1 – Medicare Data for Calendar Year 2016, page 10; Page 29

27.   The State Funding Gap: 2016, The Pew Charitable Trusts, April 2016. https://www.pewtrusts.org/-/media/assets/2018/04/state_pensions_funding_gap_2016_final.pdf

28.   The United States Census Bureau, Quick Facts, New Jersey. https://www.census.gov/quickfacts/fact/table/NJ/SBO001212

29.   Ranking of States Fiscal Condition, Mercatus Center, George Mason University, 2018. https://www.mercatus.org/publications/urban-economics/state-fiscal-rankings

30.   Age Band Compression Under Health Care Reform, Contingencies M January February 2013, Kurt Giesa and Chris Carlson. Page 33. http://www.contingenciesonline.com/contingenciesonline/20130102?pg=33#pg33

31. Want to Reduce Federal Spending? Repeal Obamacare's Steep Levies on Young People, Avik Roy, Nov 21, 2012; Forbes Magazine. https://www.forbes.com/sites/theapothecary/2012/11/21/want-to-reduce-federal-spending-repeal-obamacares-steep-levies-on-young-people/#6403571a2178

32. The State of Age Discrimination and Older Workers in the U.S. 50 years after the Age Discrimination in Employment Act , Victoria Lipnic, Acting Chair, U.S. Equal Employment Opportunity Commission. https://www.eeoc.gov/eeoc/history/adea50th/upload/report.pdf

33. Why the EEOC is zealous on age discrimination, Chris Farrell, Marketwatch Aug 27, 2018, https://www.marketwatch.com/story/why-the-eeoc-is-zealous-on-age-discrimination-2018-08-27

34. U.S. students' academic achievement still lags that of their peers in many other countries, Drew DESILVER, Pew Research. https://www.pewresearch.org/fact-tank/2017/02/15/u-s-students-internationally-math-science/

35. Ourworldindata.org; University of Oxford, Max Roser- Founder and Editor; https://ourworldindata.org/global-rise-of-education

36. World University Rankings 2018, The Times. https://www.timeshighereducation.com/world-university-rankings/2018/world-ranking#!/page/0/length/25/sort_by/rank/sort_order/asc/cols/stats

37. QS World University Rankings, 2018. https://www.topuniversities.com/university-rankings/world-university-rankings/2018

38. Academic Ranking of the Top Universities, Shanghai Ranking 2019. http://www.shanghairanking.com/

39. The Graduate Student Debt Review: The State of Graduate Student Borrowing, Jason Delisle, 2014. https://static.newamerica.org/attachments/750-the-graduate-student-debt-review/GradStudentDebtReview-Delisle-Final.pdf

40. Federal Reserve Bank of New York; Raji Chakrabarti, Andrew Haughwout, Donghoon Lee, Joelle Scally, Wilbert van Der Klaauw; Press Briefing on Household Debt, with Focus on Student Debt, April 3,2017.

41. The Condition of Education, A letter from the Commissioner, The National Center for Education Statistics, https://nces.ed.gov/programs/coe/indicator_tub.asp.

42. Office of the Under Secretary, Department of Education, Weighing the Cost and Value of a College Decision, Posted on July 24, 2013 by Courtney Clemmons; https://sites.ed.gov/ous/2013/07/weighing-the-cost-and-value-of-a-college-decision/

43. *The number of people defaulting on federal loans is rising,* Danielle Douglas-Gabriel. September 28.2017. The Washington Post. https://www.washingtonpost.com/news/grade-point/wp/2017/09/28/the-number-of-people-defaulting-on-federal-student-loans-is-climbing/?noredirect=on

44. Giving to Colleges up 6% in 2017, Heather Joselyn, The Chronicle of Philanthropy. https://www.philanthropy.com/article/Donations-to-Colleges-Up-6-in/242441

45. NCAA Finances 2017-18, Steve Berkowitz and John Kelly, USA Today, https://sports.usatoday.com/ncaa/finances/

46. NFL took in $13 billion in revenue last season — see how it stacks up against other pro sports leagues; Stephen Kutz, MarketWatch

July 2, 2016. https://www.marketwatch.com/story/the-nfl-made-13-billion-last-season-see-how-it-stacks-up-against-other-leagues-2016-07-01

47. NCAA Recruiting Fact Sheet, March 2018. https://www.ncaa.org/sites/default/files/Recruiting%20Fact%20Sheet%20WEB.pdf

48. The Likelihood of Someone Becoming a Professional Sports Player, Patrick Gleeson, PhD, Houston Chronicle, June 27, 2018; https://work.chron.com/likelihood-someone-becoming-professional-sports-player-26110.html

49. 2016 National Basketball Association Racial and Gender Report Card, Sports Business News July 14, 2016. http://www.sportsbusinessnews.com/node/36737

50. NCAA Sport Sponsorship, Participation and Demographics Search Database. http://web1.ncaa.org/rgdSearch/exec/saSearch

51. Average Athletic Scholarship per College Athlete, SholarshipStats.org, 2017. http://www.scholarshipstats.com/average-per-athlete.html

52. Estimates of the Unauthorized Immigrant Population Residing in the United States: January 2014, Department of Homeland Security, Bryan Baker. https://www.dhs.gov/sites/default/files/publications/Unauthorized%20Immigrant%20Population%20Estimates%20in%20the%20US%20January%202014_1.pdf

53. Profile of the Unauthorized Population of United States, Migration Policy Institute. https://www.migrationpolicy.org/data/unauthorized-immigrant-population/state/US

54. Draft Lottery (1969), Wikipedia. https://en.wikipedia.org/wiki/Draft_lottery_(1969)

55. An Overview of Past Pornography Rulings by the U.S. Supreme Court, Frontline, WGBH-TV Public Broadcasting Service. https://www.pbs.org/wgbh/pages/frontline/shows/porn/prosecuting/overview.html

56. Ourworldindata.org; University of Oxford, Max Roser- Founder and Editor; https://ourworldindata.org/drug-use

57. Provisional Drug Overdose Death Counts, National Center for Health Statistics, Center for Disease Control and Prevention. https://www.cdc.gov/nchs/nvss/vsrr/drug-overdose-data.htm

58. United States military casualties of war, Wikipedia. https://en.wikipedia.org/wiki/United_States_military_casualties_of_war

59. Millennial generation has no specific defined time period but generally recognized as those born between early to middle 1980's to late 1990's to early 2000's. That definition covers 20 years of births and those who would be 19 – 39 years old at the time this was written.

60. Poll: Nearly Half Of Millennials Prefer Socialism To Capitalism, Bre Payton, November 1, 2017. https://thefederalist.com/2017/11/01/study-nearly-half-millennials-prefer-socialism-capitalism/

61. Athenian Democracy, Routledge, 2005, p. 74, John Thorley, https://books.google.com/books?id=iU6EAgAAQBAJ&pg=PA74#v=onepage&q&f=false

62. The Tradition of Ancient Greek Democracy and Its Importance for Modern Democracy, Mogens Herman Hansen. https://books.google.com/books?id=8lPaSAnZg28C&lpg=PA10&vq=%22it%20would%20be%20misleading%20%22&dq=athenian%20democracy%20romanrepublic&pg=PA11#v=onepage&q&f=false

63. Commentaries on the Laws of England in Four Books, vol. 1 [1753], pgs. 123-125, Sir William Blackstone, https://oll.liberty-fund.org/titles/blackstone-commentaries-on-the-laws-of-england-in-four-books-vol-1

64. 'Iron Tears,' a British View of American Revolution, Professor Stanley Weintraub, July 3, 2005. NPR interview with Liane Hansen. https://www.npr.org/templates/transcript/transcript.php?storyId=4727956?storyId=4727956

65. Constitution of the State of South Carolina 1778, https://avalon.law.yale.edu/18th_century/sc02.asp.

66. An Act for the relief of Jews in Maryland, passed 26 February 1825, Archives of Maryland, Volume 3183, Page 1670, 26 February 1825, retrieved 5 December 2007

67. Randy J. Sparks, Africans in the Old South: Mapping Exceptional Lives Across the Atlantic World (Harvard University Press, 2016), p. 80.

68. Slave Voyages v2.2.7, Explore the Dispersal of Enslaved Africans Across the Atlantic World, https://www.slavevoyages.org/assessment/estimates

69. Human Trafficking Facts, https://polarisproject.org/human-trafficking/facts

70. New ILO Global Estimate of Forced Labour: 20.9 million victims, InternationalLabourOrganization.http://www.ilo.org/global/about-the-ilo/newsroom/news/WCMS_182109/lang--en/index.htm

71. David Brion Davis, Inhuman Bondage. The Rise and Fall of Slavery in the New World, Oxford University Press, 2006, ISBN 0195140737, p. 263.

72. The Economics of the Civil War Roger L. Ransom, University of California, Riverside; https://eh.net/encyclopedia/the-economics-of-the-civil-war/

73. Gunderson, Gerald. "The Origin of the American Civil War." Journal of Economic History 34 (1974): 915-950.

74. Goldin, Claudia Dale. "The Economics of Emancipation." Journal of Economic History 33 (1973): 66-85.

75. Ransom, Roger L. "The Economic Consequences of the American Civil War." In The Political Economy of War and Peace, edited by M. Wolfson. Norwell, MA: Kluwer Academic Publishers, 1998.

76. Professor James Downs. "Color blindness in the demographic death toll of the Civil War". University of Connecticut, April 13th 2012. "The rough 19th century estimate was that 60,000 former slaves died from the epidemic, but doctors treating black patients often claimed that they were unable to keep accurate records due to demands on their time and the lack of manpower and resources. The surviving records only include the number of black patients whom doctors encountered; tens of thousands of other slaves who died had no contact with army doctors, leaving no records of their deaths."

77. U.S. Population Census 1860 and 1870; https://www.census.gov/prod/www/decennial.html

78.   History of Woman Suffrage, Elizabeth Cady Stanton, Susan B. Anthony, Matilda Joslyn Cage, https://archive.org/stream/histo ryofwomansu02stanuoft#page/598/mode/2up

79.   Woman Suffrage, Mary Schons, National Geographic, January 21, 2011 https://www.nationalgeographic.org/news/woman-suffrage/

80.   https://suffragistmemorial.org/carrie-chapman-catt-1859-1947/

81.   How World War 1 helped give U.S. Women the Right to Vote, Dr. Kayleen Hughes, U.S. Army History Office, 2017. https://www.army.mil/article/192727/how_world_ war_i_helped_give_us_women_the_right_to_vote

82.   National Vital Statistics Reports, Births: Final Data for 2013, published January 15, 2015 https://www.cdc.gov/nchs/data/nvsr/ nvsr64/nvsr64_01.pdf

83.   Progress Cleaning the Air and Improving People's Health, Environmental Protection Agency, https://www.epa.gov/clean-air-act-overview/progress-cleaning-air-and-improving-peoples-health

84.   Ehrlich, Paul R. (1968). The Population Bomb. Ballantine Books.

85.   Global Extreme Poverty, Max Roser and Esteban Ortiz-Ospina, OurWorldinData.org, March 27,2017; https://ourworldindata. org/extreme-poverty

86.   https://ourworldindata.org/uploads/2019/04/Extreme-Poverty-projection-by-the-World-Bank-to-2030.png

87.   Sources of Growth in Crop Production, Food and Agriculture Organization of the United Nations. http://www.fao.org/3/ y4252e/y4252e06.htm

88. OurworldinData.org, University of Oxford, Max Roser- Founder and Editor; https://ourworldindata.org/extreme-poverty

89. National Assessment of Nations Progress https://www.nationsre-portcard.gov/reading_math_g12_2013/#/about

90. Asian Immigrants in the United States, Jie Zong and Jeanne Batalova, Migration Policy Institute. https://www.migrationpolicy.org/article/asian-immigrants-united-states#Income%20and%20 Povert

91. Marjorie Spruill Wheeler (1993). New Women of the New South: The Leaders of the Woman Suffrage Movement in the Southern States. Oxford University Press. p. 25.

92. Big Business is Getting Bigger, Andrew Flowers, The FiveThirtyEight Podcast, ABC News. https://fivethirtyeight.com/fcaturcs/big-busincss-is-gctting-bigger/

93. TobaccoRelatedMortality,CentersForDiseaseControlandPrevention. https://www.cdc.gov/tobacco/data_statistics/fact_sheets/ health_effects/tobacco_related_mortality/index.htm

94. The history of the discovery of the cigarette–lung cancer link: evidentiary traditions, corporate denial, global toll. Robert N. Proctor, BMJ Journals. https://tobaccocontrol.bmj.com/content/21/2/87

95. Marketing Violent Entertainment to Children: A Review of Self-Regulation and Industry Practices in the Motion Picture, Music Recording & Electronic Game Industries, U.S. Federal Trade Commission, 2000. https://www.ftc.gov/system/files/documents/ reports/marketing-violent-entertainment-children-review-self-regulation-industry-practices-motion-picture/vioreport.pdf

96. Policy Statement—Media Violence, American Academy of Pediatrics, 2009. https://pediatrics.aappublications.org/content/pediatrics/124/5/1495.full.pdf

97. The Influence of Media Violence on Youth, Craig A. Anderson, Leonard Berkowitz, Edward Donnerstein, et al, Journal of Psychological Science in the Public Interest, December 1, 2003. https://journals.sagepub.com/doi/10.1111/j.1529-1006.2003.pspi_1433.x

98. Longitudinal Relations Between Children's Exposure to TV Violence and Their Aggressive and Violent Behavior in Young Adulthood: 1977–1992, L. Rowell Huesmann, Jessica Moise-Titus, Cheryl-Lynn Podolski, and Leonard D. Eron, Developmental Psychology, Vol 39, 2003 pgs. 201-221. https://www.apa.org/pubs/journals/releases/dev-392201.pdf

99. The Impact of Electronic Media Violence: Scientific Theory and Research, L. Rowell Hausmann, December 2007, Journal of Adolescent Health. https://www.jahonline.org/article/S1054-139X(07)00391-6/fulltext

100. Short-term and Long-term Effects of Violent Media on Aggression in Children and Adults, Brad J. Bushman, PhD; L. Rowell Huesmann, PhD, JAMA Pediatrics, April 2006. https://jamanetwork.com/journals/jamapediatrics/fullarticle/204790

101. Regulation of Public Sector Collective Bargaining in the States, Milla Sanes and John Schmitt, Center for Economic and Policy Research, 2014. http://cepr.net/documents/state-public-cb-2014-03.pdf

102. Government employment: an era of slow growth Office of Employment Structure and Trends, Bureau of Labor Statistics,

MONTHLY LABOR REVIEW October 1981 JOHN T. TUCKER, https://stats.bls.gov/opub/mlr/1981/10/art3full.pdf

103. Cory Booker Turns on His One-Time Ally, Betsy DeVos. Ian Tuttle, The National Review, February 8, 2017. https://www. nationalreview.com/2017/02/cory-booker-betsy-devos-statement-hypocritical-school-choice-teachers-union-education/

104. Newspapers Fact Sheet, Pew Research Center: Journalism and Media. https://www.journalism.org/fact-sheet/newspapers/

105. The American Journalist in the Digital Age: Key Findings, Lars Willnat and David H. Weaver, School of Journalism, Indiana University. http://archive.news.indiana.edu/releases/iu/2014/05/2013-american-journalist-key-findings.pdf

Made in the USA
Middletown, DE
11 February 2020